PROPHETIC, POST-APOSTOLIC & POSTMODERN

An Oriental Approach to Three Bible Studies

Smyth & Helwys Publishing, Inc.
6316 Peake Road
Macon, Georgia 31210-3960
1-800-747-3016
©2009 by Smyth & Helwys Publishing
All rights reserved.
Printed in the United States of America.

The paper used in this publication meets the minimum requirements of
American National Standard for Information Sciences—
Permanence of Paper for Printed Library Materials.
ANSI Z39.48–1984. (alk. paper)

Library of Congress Cataloging-in-Publication Data

Prophetic, post-apostolic & postmodern:
Three Bible studies from a missionary to Japan /
by Charles Whaley. p. cm.
Includes bibliographical references and index.
ISBN 978-1-57312-548-2 (pbk. : alk. paper)
1. Bible. N.T. Peter—Criticism, interpretation, etc.
2. Bible. O.T. Job—Criticism, interpretation, etc.
3. Bible. O.T. Jeremiah—Criticism, interpretation, etc.
I. Title. II. Title: Prophetic, post-apostolic, and postmodern.
BS2795.52.W53 2009 220.6—dc22 2009044683

Cover art: *Called* by Lois Whaley. Lois titled her picture *Called* because it features
three swans going in different directions but all turning toward the sound of a voice from the shore.
It was meant to depict how God's call comes to Christians at different phases of their lives.

Disclaimer of Liability: With respect to statements of opinion or fact available in this work of nonfiction, Smyth & Helwys Publishing Inc. nor any of its employees, makes any warranty, express or implied, or assumes any legal liability or responsibility for the accuracy or completeness of any information disclosed, or represents that its use would not infringe privately-owned rights.

Prophetic, Post-apostolic & Postmodern

AN ORIENTAL APPROACH TO THREE BIBLE STUDIES

CHARLES WHALEY

Dedication

This book is dedicated to the Christians of Japan whose sacrificial witness amid a non-Christian environment challenges believers everywhere to strive for deeper levels of faith and Christian action.

Preface

After spending forty-three years working with schools and churches across Japan, I tend to see things through Japanese eyes and have added that perspective to these studies of three pivotal books in the Bible. They include insights and illustrations gleaned from my years in Japan and are designed to bring new depth and meaning to one's understanding of the Old and New Testaments.

The book of Jeremiah holds the prophet's magnificent Temple Sermon that has inspired Japanese Christians to become today's prophets, courageously challenging the secular and religious status quo. The book of Job captures the search for meaning and hope experienced by Christian minorities across the world as they struggle with the problems of righteous suffering. First and 2 Peter are about a post-apostolic Christianity that holds important lessons for today's postmodern church.

These three Bible studies were presented at Decatur First Baptist Church and other Atlanta area churches over the past five years and are published here with the hope that they may add depth and objectivity to the study of God's word.

I am indebted to Dr. Vera Campbell Gullatt for the valuable time she spent proofreading the final manuscript and to the staff at Smyth & Helwys for their exceptionally kind and professional manner of readying the book for publication.

—Charles Whaley

Contents

Preface 2

1 & 2 Peter
Chapter 1   Post-apostolic & Postmodern 7
Chapter 2   Strangers & Aliens 15
Chapter 3   The People of God 21
Chapter 4   The Two Ways 29
Chapter 5   The Blood of Martyrs 35
Chapter 6   Sound Doctrine 43

Job
Chapter 7   Tragedy & Triumph in Job 49
Chapter 8   The Question 55
Chapter 9   Divine Justice 61
Chapter 10 Signs of Recovery 67
Chapter 11 The Final Answer 73

Jeremiah
Chapter 12 Jeremiah: Prophet to the Nations 79
Chapter 13 A Global Mission 85
Chapter 14 Broken Marriage Syndrome 91
Chapter 15 Temple Sermon 97
Chapter 16 The Pain of God 103
Chapter 17   A Letter from Home 109
Chapter 18 A New Covenant 113

Appendix: A Unique Theological Heritage
"Tell it to the Church" (Origin) 121
"Tear Down Those Walls" (Conflicts) 129
"Saved by His Life" (Nature) 137

Chapter 1

Post-apostolic & Postmodern

The second stage of any movement is never easy, and Christianity is no exception. We call the age in which the General Epistles were written *post-apostolic* because the original gospel founders were gone and believers had to face an increasingly hostile non-Christian world. Jesus and the apostles were no longer present to give needed leadership and advice as Christians faced misunderstanding and persecution. Churches also had to deal with internal heresies that threatened to destroy them from within. The future of Christianity depended on whether they could survive and witness in the most dangerous period of Christian history.

Generally, most believers today are familiar with the Protestant Reformation and understand their denomination's early American beginnings. They also know the broad outlines of biblical history, but they have little knowledge of what happened during the intervening period. That's especially true of the post-apostolic age of the great church fathers, the time before an official canon of Scripture was finalized.

I'm convinced that post-apostolic Christianity holds important messages for postmodern believers because today's church is in another second stage movement fraught with many of the same issues that first-century Christians faced. Believers today struggle to rescue a stagnant church without the help of Reformation giants such as Martin Luther or American Christian pioneers such as Georgia's own Daniel Marshall.

A recent issue of the *New York Times* featured a front-page article about the church's loss of teenagers. It estimated that only 4 percent of today's teens would be active Christians as adults, compared with 35 percent of current baby boomers and 65 percent of the World War II generation.[1] Even Billy Graham's book *The Journey* tells how he, once a robust evangelist, now has to use a walker.[2] I read it with the sad realization that one age of the church is swiftly passing and with a prayer for God to fortify contemporary Christians with the same dynamic faith that enabled post-apostolic believers to survive in their world.

For this first section we're going to focus primarily on the vital statistics for 1 and 2 Peter: writers, dates, recipients, issues and how these relate to present-day Christianity. In an effort to get at the universal truths of these two epistles, we'll try to understand the specific context in which they were written. And in order to avoid the risk of getting bogged down in a detailed verse-by-verse study, we'll concentrate on certain representative passages.

The two epistles of Peter speak to present day Christianity as they address the complex issues of transition to a new age in the first century. They offer the same hope to present day believers that they did to the early Christians that the persecutions had scattered throughout the Roman Empire. Believers at that time were fighting on two fronts. On one hand, they were struggling against outward threats of death and misunderstanding and on the other hand they were facing threats of perversion and disunity within the church itself. The two epistles held just the encouragement those early Christians needed to survive and to witness in such an age. They restated the basic tenets of biblical faith; they retold the true nature of the church; they urged believers to observe Christian ethical standards, even in an age of transition, and they promised hope to those who kept the faith. As circular letters they were passed among believers across the Roman Empire. It is impossible to overstate the importance of these letters to the survival of the early church in those dark and difficult times.

Who wrote the two letters? First Peter clearly states that the apostle himself wrote that epistle but the letter's contents, its date of writing, and its excellent Greek language give reason to doubt that claim. Since it was hardly possible for an uneducated Galilean fisherman like Peter to have written such excellent Greek and because the letter's contents were about events that happened after Peter's death, it is reasonable to assume that the letter was written by one of Peter's followers instead of by the apostle himself. Sylvanias—or Silas, which is the Aramaic pronunciation of that name—the apostle's trusted helper mentioned in chapter 5, is the prime candidate for such a writer. Not only was he capable of writing the epistle's excellent Greek, he was much younger than Peter and could have written it after the apostle's death.

Second Peter is entirely different from 1 Peter in language, structure, date, and style. Its very first verse ascribes a rare name to Peter, calling him Simeon instead of Simon: "Simeon Peter, a servant and apostle of Jesus Christ" (l:1). Since most scholars agree that this epistle is too late to have been written by the apostle himself, it is generally thought that a Hellenized Jewish Christian from the famous Petrine school in Rome wrote it following the apostle's death. Also, the epistles of 2 Peter and Jude are virtually identical, as can be seen by comparing chapters 2 and 3 in 2 Peter with v. 6-18 in Jude. This is likely not due to outright copying but to the fact that both writers used a common source.

It would be a serious mistake, however, to conclude that the apostle Peter has no relation to the two epistles since he is not likely their author. His towering presence is everywhere in both letters, sounding a fresh and unique understanding of the gospel and the church. Peter's dramatic conversion experience and the faith content of his sermons are woven into the salvation theology that dominates the epistles' doctrinal statements. The apostle's famous faith confession to Christ and his part in the church's beginning at Pentecost are seen in the two letters' dynamic image of a New Testament church. First Peter even invokes Peter's definition of the *koinonia*, as the people of God. Further, the apostle's experiences of denial and forgiveness add a vital human touch that characterizes the epistles' sections on morality. And Peter's presence with Jesus at the transfiguration and the resurrection give the two letters a divine touch that has inspired readers through the ages. Finally, the apostle's pioneer mission ministry to the

Gentiles accounts for a Gentile emphasis found throughout both letters. No doubt about it; Peter's unseen presence is felt throughout the epistles, making them two of the most meaningful and important books in the entire New Testament.

Where were the epistles written? In 1 Peter 5 the place of writing for that letter is identified as Babylon, a code name early Christians used for Rome: "Your sister church in Babylon sends you greetings." Second Peter's place of writing is unknown.

Who were the recipients of these letters? First Peter is addressed to "exiles of the dispersion" or believers in, "Pontus, Galatia, Cappadocia, Asia, and Bithynia." In other words they were Diaspora believers who had gone there to escape the severe persecutions in Palestine and who now desperately needed pastoral leadership and encouragement to maintain their faith in a foreign setting. The second epistle's readers were mainly Gentile converts, "those who received faith of equal standing." They were believed to be people of Hellenistic culture well versed in the Greek language.

When were the epistles written? The most likely scenario for 1 Peter is that someone else wrote the letter using Peter's name. In that case, the date of writing would have been quite late. Most scholars place it sometime during the latter part of the first century. If the apostle himself wrote 1 Peter, it would have been earlier, say 67 CE. Tradition places Peter's martyrdom in the mid 60s. Second Peter was written even later. Chapter 3 notes the passing of an age of the apostles, "ever since our ancestors died" (3:4), observing that a new age was just beginning. Also the epistle's writer implores readers to remember the commandments "from the apostles." This and other evidence places 2 Peter's date of writing about the middle of the second century (130–160 CE).

The General Epistles were written about the same time as a host of extra-biblical literature and need to be distinguished from the latter. Dan Brown, the famous novelist, shook up the Christian world when he reached back to Gnostic literature of this period for *The Da Vinci Code*. His novel generated so much interest in so-called New Age literature that now Gnostic Gospels jam the shelves of bookstores everywhere. However, the major problem with the *The Da Vinci Code* and similar books is that they place Gnostic literature on the same level with the books in the New Testament. Yet they fail to cite the criticism of such apocryphal works by responsible contemporary scholars such as Iraneus. Consequently many people come away from these novels with questionable conclusions about the life of Christ. Incidentally, there are numerous other extra-biblical works about the apostle Peter in *The Apocryphal New Testament* (published by Oxford University Press). They are an excellent reference for further study of Gnostic Gospels.

One has to remember that 1 and 2 Peter belong to the New Testament canon, adopted by the council of Nicaea in 325 CE, that has withstood the test of time. Unfortunately, the canon wasn't finalized until the fourth century because Christians had previously been forbidden to assemble and were unable to meet and evaluate all the literature available during the three hundred years of persecution. That meant that believers during that time had to sort through all sorts of extra-biblical writings and decide for themselves what was authentic and what was not.

Doctrinal sections of 1 and 2 Peter are based on a set of early Christian doctrines known as the *Kerygma* and sections on morality that reflect the ethical principles found in an early church handbook called the *Didache*. The former is a name given to the theology that is found in Peter's sermons in Acts. The latter is a believer's handbook which dates all the way back to the first century. We shall discuss both of these writings in later sections of this study.

Unfortunately, the two New Testament books are not without their difficulties. Although 1 Peter begins with a forceful reminder of the great Christian doctrines and ethical codes, the account of Jesus' descent into Hades (3:19-20; 4:6) is what Barkley, the famous New Testament scholar, calls the most difficult passage in the entire New Testament. That's because it poses all sorts of questions about what Jesus was doing in Hades. The *Apostles Creed*, quoted regularly in worship services around the globe, even mentions it in the passage: "He descended into Hell; the third day he rose again from the dead." How does one resolve the difficulty of this passage? One interpretation is that its key word "announcement" (κερησσειν), suggests a triumphant pronouncement of victory over evil that Jesus made to heavenly beings following his resurrection. Again, there is always the allegorical interpretation that sees this episode as symbolic, similar to events in the book of Revelation.

Despite the trials of faith in 1 and 2 Peter an unmistakable note of victory runs throughout. Primarily, the two epistles are about encouragement, challenge, hope and victory. Assurance that the severe testing is not without meaning is found in such passages as the following one in 1 Peter: "You know that your tried and tested faith, more precious than gold refined by fire, will be changed into glory when Jesus comes" (l:7). Whether it is the first century or the twenty-first century, that's what makes one's faith struggle worthwhile.

My favorite story from the post-apostolic era is that of Ignatius who was pastor of the Antioch church in Palestine at the turn of the first century. Arrested for preaching the gospel, he was sentenced to be executed in the coliseum in Rome. The court assigned two Roman guards to accompany him there and together they set out on a journey to the Eternal City. When they passed through the region of Cappacodia, north of Palestine, they found so many Diaspora Christians who had gone there to escape persecution that Ignatius requested permission to meet with them. The guards agreed and this great man of God visited one Diaspora church after another, preaching, teaching, meeting with church leaders and counseling those in need for a truly wonderful ministry to displaced people who were lonely and hungry for Christian fellowship.

But the exciting thing about that trip was what happened when they reached the port city of Smyrna. While he waited for the ship that would take him to his execution in Rome, Ignatius sat down and wrote seven letters to the churches he had just visited. And wonder of wonders, we still have those letters today. They give me goose bumps every time I read them and ponder the depth of courage and faith they represent. What could Ignatius who was en route to his own martyrdom possibly say to those Christians in exile? They were believers who had left home to escape persecution themselves and were living under the constant fear of death. Would Ignatius say to them, "You too will be executed unless you recant your faith?" Not at all. Read the letters yourself. Hope is written across every page, and from beginning to end the letters are filled with messages of encouragement and hope, and with the challenge to stand fast in one's faith, no matter what.

No one expected the church to survive those years of trial and suffering. But guess what! After three hundred years of the most severe persecutions of Christians ever, once religious freedom was established, people were amazed to discover that over one third of the Roman Empire had become Christian. Even emperor Constantine told of praying to the Christian God before an important battle. He reported seeing a cross in the sky with the words *hoc signor vince* ("conquer by this sign") written underneath and became a believer himself. That's when he issued the Edict of Milan that freed Christians there once and for all.

The two epistles of 1 and 2 Peter point the way to survival, witness and victory for Christians in any age. May God help us respond today with renewed faith, dedication, and action.

Notes

1. Laurie Goodstein, "Evangelicals Fear the Loss of Their Teenagers," *New York Times*, 6 October 2006.

2. Billy Graham, *The Journey: Living by Faith in an Uncertain World* (Nashville: Nelson, 2006).

Chapter 2

Strangers & Aliens

In Japan I had to apply for an alien registration certificate and was told that I had to carry it with me at all times as long as I remained in that country. It contained my photo, my fingerprints and other vital personal data that identified me as an outsider, an alien, someone who didn't belong there. At first I was so ashamed of the document that I didn't take seriously the directive to carry it with me everywhere I went. But one day an officer stopped me and asked to see my registration card and when he learned that I had left it at home, he took me to the police station downtown. Lois and I had gone on a shopping spree in the community that day and he let her go because she had her card in her purse. But the trip turned into a nightmare for me, with a humiliating day of long grilling from the authorities. After that, I was never without that alien identification card during the forty-three years I spent in Japan. It was a constant reminder that I was a foreigner, an outsider, an alien, a person away from home.

The writer of 1 Peter addresses his letter to strangers and aliens as he begins an epistle of crisis theology for believers on the run. That's what he called Christians scattered across the Roman empire: *Diaspora aliens*. It's the same thing they'd called me in Japan—an alien. Originally the word *Diaspora* was used to describe the Jewish people that Assyrians and Babylonians had taken captive during Old Testament times. But 1 Peter uses it here for first-century Christians, both Jews and Gentiles who had left home to escape persecution. Many of them sought refuge in Cappadocia north of Palestine where they lived in mountain caves, keeping constant vigil for forces out to kill Christians.

These first-century Christians were severely persecuted because society grossly misunderstood their faith and treated them as criminals. For one thing, government authorities misinterpreted their loyalty to the kingdom of God as treason against the Roman government. Also, the Eucharist ceremony—the practice of drinking blood and eating the body of Christ—was viewed as a form of cannibalism. Even attendance at regular worship services was seen as a subversive activity since participation in secret meetings was forbidden by law. Justin Martyr, one of my favorite personalities from that period, was a Christian lawyer from Palestine who gave his life in 120 CE defending the faith against such false charges. He belonged to a group of Apologists, who used the word *logos*, a favorite term of Greek philosophers, to explain the gospel to non-Christians.

In such a setting as this it was impossible to be a nominal Christian. Believers then had to be absolutely certain that what they believed was worth the sacrifice of their lives. They desperately needed a crisis theology by which to live and to die.

The short statement of faith at the beginning of 1 Peter is precisely that kind of crisis theology. It's based on the faith expressed in Peter's sermons to the early church. C. H. Dodd, a world-renowned theologian, identified five preaching points from the apostle's New Testament messages as first-century Christian doctrines. He called them *kerygma* (κερνσσο), or preaching points, after the Greek verb for preaching. Not surprisingly, these five principles of the *kerygma* are those that form the theology found in 1 Peter. After all, it is an epistle about Peter's faith. The five points are as follows:

1. Jesus is the fulfillment of Old Testament prophecy.
2. His death on the cross inaugurates a new era of the Spirit.
3. His resurrection makes him Messiah, Lord and head of the new Israel.
4. He promises to come again soon.
5. This gospel is the basis for repentance, forgiveness and salvation.

The brief doctrinal statement that begins the epistle of 1 Peter is absolutely exciting because it wraps Christian beliefs around the various dimensions of salvation. To me, the entire passage is an overview of what salvation means. It's a dynamic theology for believers in crisis, a doctrine for people on the run. Let's call it *theologia viatorum*, a living theology that can be identified in the following ways:

First, the epistle says that salvation is a birth experience where God breaths new life into an individual and makes that person into a new creation: "You have been born anew, not of perishable but of imperishable seed, through the living and enduring word of God" (1:23). The Greek word for *born anew* in this passage, αναγεννησας, is found only twice in the New Testament. However, Jesus used a similar expression that means virtually the same thing, when he told Nicodemus that in order to enter the kingdom of God he would have to be born again (γεννηθαι ανωθεν). The doctrine of new birth here is the same as that found throughout the New Testament.

You heard right! Belief in the new birth is precisely that: a doctrine. In fact, it is one of the most potent and unique doctrines in the New Testament. To the writer of 1 Peter, salvation meant something more than intellectual assent to a set of philosophical principles. It signified a birth process when one was born into the new and wonderful world of the Spirit. I have a book by the respected theologian Harold DeWolf titled *A Theology of the Living Church* (New York: Harper & Row, 1968) that has a whole chapter on the doctrine of New Birth. The writer is a progressive theologian who explains the new birth in psychological, ethical and theological terms as a transformation absolutely essential to the Christian faith.

Christians across the Orient dearly love the word *new birth* and use its Chinese character *shinsei* to name everything imaginable: churches, evangelistic campaigns and publications. In Japanese history, when people were ready to write down their language, they borrowed characters from the Chinese who'd already developed an elaborate system of writing. But the Japanese gave those Chinese characters Japanese pronunciations and used them to write the Japanese language. That means, of course, that the characters now have both Chinese and Japanese pronunciations. Thus, the Chinese reading of *shin sei*, or new life, can also be read in Japanese *atarashiku umareru* or born anew.

Oriental Christians feel that New Birth theology distinguishes their faith from traditional Oriental religious thought. For instance, the Buddhist practice of enlightenment, an intellectual process of intensive meditation aimed at ridding the mind of desire, is more a philosophy than a religion per se. Buddhist literature is even catalogued as philosophy and carried in that section in Japanese libraries. New birth theology, however, teaches that the gospel is more than a mental exercise; it is a whole new way of life for those born from above (Gal 6:15).

Next, the epistle depicts salvation as a new covenant relationship with the divine. First Peter borrows the phrase "Sprinkled with blood" (1:2), from the Old Testament to describe what happens in a conversion experience. It refers to the way Moses sprinkled animal blood on the altar in order to seal the covenant at Sinai. But "sprinkled with blood" in 1 Peter isn't about animal blood at all rather; it refers to the spiritual bond of the new covenant that Jesus' sacrificial death seals between the believer and the Lord. It's a bond that Peter himself experienced in his dramatic conversion recorded in Acts 9.

The epistle of 1 Peter also describes salvation as living hope: "He has given us new birth into a living hope through the resurrection of Jesus Christ" (1:3). In other words, it says that Christian hope is based on one's resurrection faith. In his letter to the Colossians, Paul wrote: "If you have been raised with Christ, seek the things that are above" (Col 3:1). Hope is what early Christians desperately needed as they faced possible death for their beliefs. It is difficult for people who are satisfied with the luxuries of this life to know the depths of spiritual hope that the gospel held for those who had nothing else. Such a joy of anticipation is reserved for those who are willing to sacrifice everything for what they believe.

Again, 1 Peter says that salvation guarantees the believer a new spiritual heritage (1:4). Here, the Greek word for inheritance is similar to the Old Testament Hebrew for the promised land or the land of inheritance. But the inheritance alluded to in 1 Peter is vastly superior to a mere piece of land. Salvation here is about becoming heir to an inheritance that lasts forever Not only that, Paul adds that it makes one a *joint heir* with Christ himself (Rom 8:17).

When I was chancellor at our Baptist University in Fukuoka I was shocked to learn Japan's strict laws regarding inheritance. I had proposed to our trustee board that we set up an endowment fund and encourage friends of the institution to will their assets to our school. That is the way private universities are funded in the U.S. But the plan fell flat when the school lawyers informed me that Japan's laws governing inheritance prohibit people from donating their assets to anyone or anything outside the family, including one's extended family. When someone dies in Japan the entire estate must go to the children or other qualified family members. Rome's inheritance laws, to which this Scripture refers, were similar. It was unthinkable for a person's assets to go to anyone or anything other than one's family.

In this opening section, the writer of 1 Peter depicts salvation as a lifelong growth process where one is born not just once but continually, day by day. Further, concerning the goal of salvation he writes, "As the outcome (*telos* or target) of your faith, you obtain the salvation of your souls" (1:9). Does that mean salvation is complete only in heaven? I think it does! The epistle even goes on to say that the result of this New Birth experience is so glorious that even the angels "long to look" (1:12).

Early Christians accepted their outsider status and believers do so again today for one reason: they're convinced that what they believe is more valuable than life itself. Their faith is their treasure; it's like that which made Jesus' parable come alive when he said, "The kingdom of heaven is like a treasure hidden in a field, which someone found—then in his joy he goes and sells all that he has and buys that field" (Matt 13:44). Again he said, "Where your treasure is, there will your heart be also" (Luke 12:34).

A few years ago, a young seminary graduate demonstrated 1 Peter's theology as he became pastor of a small church in the remote mountain town of Safenwell Switzerland. Like many other young ministers, he began his ministry determined to preach the finest sermons ever and to conduct programs of community outreach that would cause the church to grow and bring a new spiritual atmosphere to the area. He vowed to put into practice the principles of preaching and church administration that he had learned in the seminary. But it wasn't long before he became disillusioned. Why? Despite preaching his heart out there was little response and although he visited people regularly and participated in community activities, essentially nothing changed. The church growth he had envisioned never happened. Convinced something was missing that he just could not put his finger on, he talked with other young pastors in the area and discovered that he wasn't alone in those thoughts. They, too, were having the same problem; some so frustrated they were considering leaving the ministry.

Finally, the pastors decided to meet together once a month and reread the Bible to see if there was something they'd missed. That's what they did. They met regularly and reread God's word without comment, earnestly seeking to discover the secret of the early church. As they read through the New Testament, they all began to sense a note of urgency that characterized young Christians and young churches throughout the Scriptures. They discovered a crisis mentality that saturated the early church and caused new believers to sacrifice and witness even in the face of growing opposition. This young pastor wrote it all down and eventually became the great church leader and famous theologian that we know today, as Karl Barth. And guess what they called his theology? They called it a theology of crisis or Barth's Crisis Theology.

First Peter is about rediscovering the sense of urgency; the new birth; the new relationship; the new hope, and the new spiritual heritage that we find in God's word. It says that although we're sojourners, outsiders and travelers in this world, our eternal home and our infinite treasure are in heaven with the Lord of Life.

Chapter 3

The People of God

The most popular Christian group in Japan today is a fellowship of believers called *Mukyokai*, literally *a no-church church.* It's a completely indigenous body of believers unrelated to any Western mission organization, composed primarily of intellectuals and former samurai warriors who found a home among Christians when there was no longer a place for them in Japanese society. Their members include university professors, a former president of prestigious Tokyo University, several members of the Diet, a Supreme Court Judge and numerous other intellectuals and national leaders. In lieu of baptism, new members sign a covenant of faith and in addition to Sunday worship the groups meet regularly at the noon hour on week-days to study the Bible in its original Hebrew and Greek texts. The founder, Uchimura Kanzo, is counted among Japan's most outstanding citizens. And, although Mukyokai doesn't fit the orthodox pattern for a traditional church, it has had a greater impact on Japanese society than all the imported denominations in that country.

First Peter grabs our attention in chapter 2 by calling *Diaspora* believers to unite as the people of God. But nowhere is there any mention of the word church or any organizational structure associated with that name. Instead, the author reaches back to Pentecost for a word that describes them as the people of God. In other words, 1 Peter sees the church as a fellowship rather than simply another organization.

However, even though the epistle never uses the word church, chapter 2 gives one of the most profound descriptions of a New Testament Church found anywhere in God's word. It begins with the ideal of a fellowship of believers striving to reach true spiritual maturity, "Like newborn babies, long for the pure, spiritual milk, so that by it you may grow into salvation"(2:2). What follows is a description of the church's foundation, nature and function that depicts it as a vibrant living organism, rooted and grounded in resurrection faith. This passage in 1 Peter and the Pentecost account in Acts, are two sources Bible scholars use to define a New Testament Church. Notice especially the imagery of stone and stones from Peter's name that are used to depict the true nature of the church and its members.

First, the epistle describes the church's foundation as *a living stone*, "Come to him, a living stone, though rejected by mortals, yet chosen and precious in God's sight"(2:4). This is a reference to Matthew 16, which cites Peter's faith as the rock on which Jesus built his church. Further, it points to the pivotal passage in Isaiah that says, "See, I lay a stone in Zion, a tested stone, a precious cornerstone for a sure foundation; the one who trusts will never be dismayed"(28:16). Basically, this Scripture says that the church's foundation is alive! Theologian Karl Barth explains that the church is not an abstract entity but a living organism; that is, he said it's never simply *a church* per se but must constantly become *the church* through worship and witness.

Next, 1 Peter goes on to describe the nature of the church's membership as a body of *living stones*. Here again, the word living is the key: "Like living stones, let yourself be built into a spiritual house"(2:4-5). Just as the church is founded on a living stone; its members are living stones that make the body of Christ come alive. A parallel passage in Ephesians expands on the same idea, "So you are no longer strangers and aliens, but you are citizens with the saints and also members of the household of God, built upon the foundation of the apostles and prophets, with Christ Jesus himself a the cornerstone. In him the whole structure is joined together and grows into a holy temple in the Lord; in whom you also are built together spiritually into a dwelling place for God" (Eph 2:19).

The concept that the church is alive takes me back to a decision our Japanese Baptist congregations faced when two important meetings in Tokyo coincided one beautiful Easter Sunday. One was a memorial service for Toyohiko Kagawa, the world-renowned Christian leader who had just died. I had heard him speak on numerous occasions and still have a copy of his book, *Songs from the Slums* (Cokesbury, 1935), in my study. In fact, his sacrificial ministry to the outcasts of Kobe was a major factor in my decision to become a missionary and I, along with our national Christians, wanted to be present for his final service. But a new Baptist church was being born in a Tokyo suburb that same Easter Sunday afternoon. We faced the dilemma of whether our people should attend the memorial service for Kagawa or join this small body of believers to dedicate their new church. We were torn between the two at first but finally decided on the latter, to participate in the birth of the new instead of mourning the passing of the old. We did so because we were convinced that was what Kagawa would have done as one whose whole life and ministry was centered in a living faith. And guess what? The Akatsuka Baptist Church, born that Easter Sunday afternoon, has now grown to become one of the strongest churches in all Japan. Not only was I privileged to attend its organizational service that memorable Easter Sunday, recently the church paid my way back to Japan to conduct a weeklong series of evangelistic meetings in celebration of the anniversary of its founding.

Finally, the passage uses a series of meaningful terms to capture the church's function: "A chosen race, a royal priesthood, a holy nation, God's own people."

The words chosen race remind believers that they are a people bound to the Lord and to one another in a covenant relationship with the divine the same way that the Israelites were long ago. This covenant relationship designated Diaspora Christians in the first century as God's chosen people with special blessings and responsibilities similar to those the original covenant promised to the Israelites who remained faithful to their Lord. Many churches today refer to themselves as covenant churches because they feel the word covenant best describes their special relationship to one another and to God. Basically this Scripture in 1 Peter tells us that Christians are a covenant people and that the church is their home. It's where they belong.

I like the story of a little girl who lost her way and couldn't remember how to get home. When a policeman found her sobbing on a street corner and asked where she lived, she looked up at him and said, "Oh, just take me to the church, I can find my way home from there."

Next, the church's designation as a Royal Priesthood brings to mind the Reformation principle of the priesthood of the believer. Many mistake this to mean that all believers have direct access to God and have no need for someone to intercede on their behalf. While that may be true, the term royal priesthood in 1 Peter is about a corporate priestly role that congregations engage in to minister to the people around them. It depicts the church as a shepherd to the community, to the nation and to the world.

I learned the importance of the church's priestly role when the congregation I was leading in Fukuoka built a new sanctuary. They had outgrown the house church where they met and had raised enough money to purchase land and build a sanctuary. The church building they envisioned was one that would be a unique expression of their faith. However, they were deeply disappointed to discover that the architect they chose knew absolutely nothing about a Christian church. As you can imagine, that's a problem congregations in non-Christian lands face all the time. Even undertakers in Japan often have to be told what to do when they have a Christian funeral. But after spending endless hours with the contractor, our church building committee finally came up with a set of plans they felt were satisfactory and the congregation approved them with just one condition: "We want our church to have a steeple and a bell," they said. They explained that although the church holds worship services only at specified times during the week, the building witnesses to the community twenty four hours a day, seven days a week. "We want a steeple with a cross on top which proclaims to the community this is God's house and we want the church to have a bell that lets people know this congregation is praying for them," they said. You guessed it! The church at Fukuma now has a steeple and a bell and both the building and the bell do indeed proclaim the good news of God's mighty works twenty-four seven.

The Greek word people in the phrase, *people of God*, can also be translated laymen, as if to say the church of Christ is a body of laymen, not a congregation of theologians. That is, the church stands and falls on the faith of ordinary believers. To emphasize that fact, the writer of 1 Peter quotes from Hosea saying, "Once you were not a people, but now you are God's people; once you had not received mercy, but now you have received mercy" (1 Pet 2:10). It's a passage about that prophet's broken marriage relationship with Gomer. Remember how Hosea insisted on renewing his marriage bond even though his wife was unfaithful? This is an illustration of God's love for Israel. First Peter, written mainly for Gentiles, uses that Old Testament episode to depict the church as a body of wayward people who were reconciled to God.

Finally, the epistle of 1 Peter turns to the most important question of all the church's reason for being, its *raison d'etre*. Why is the church a chosen race, a royal priesthood, a holy nation? What is its ultimate purpose and meaning? Verse 9 of this wonderful passage answers with a resounding declaration of the churches' calling: "But you are a chosen race, a royal priesthood, a holy nation, God's own people, in order that you may proclaim the mighty acts of him who called you out of darkness into his marvelous light" (2:9). That's why! Writing to Diaspora believers caught up in the struggle against persecution and heresy, the author calls on them, as people of God, to proclaim his mighty works to all people everywhere. Could this be Peter's Great Commission?

It grieves me to see congregations shying away from global missions these days. The world is more complex, I know. Modern travel and technology have brought us closer to other world faiths than ever before. And we do need to better understand other cultures and other religions. But it's clear throughout the New Testament that to be the church of God means to proclaim the gospel. And after doing just that for over forty three years in one of the world's most advanced cultures, I can testify that the response is still, absolutely phenomenal.

The image of the church as a body of living stones founded on the stone of living faith is that of a formidable force capable of impacting society with the gospel of peace and righteousness. It's the picture of a force God used to change the world through history and one that I'm confident can do it again today.

The epistle of 1 Peter is a challenge to rediscover the true nature of the New Testament church and to reclaim its mission to the world. And where better to find that image than this passage in 1 Peter and also the account of what happened at Pentecost? If churches today are to impact the twenty-first century as Diaspora churches did the first century, they need to be New Testament churches like those depicted in these two passages.

Several years ago something amazing happened when communism came to an end in a small Siberian city in Russia where people rediscovered the church and its ministry. In the wake of their newfound religious freedom, Christian worship services sprang up everywhere and people even came from abroad to have a part in the revival that was sweeping that nation. Unfortunately the people in this remote area faced a problem because no Russian Bibles could be found to use for their worship services. But as they talked, some residents remembered that the government had confiscated thousands of Bibles years ago and they began to ask what the soldiers had done with them.

Suddenly, an elderly gentleman stood up in the rear of the room and said, "I know where the Bibles are." Straightway he led a crowd of enthusiastic believers to an abandoned warehouse several miles outside of the city. The building was securely sealed and there were signs everywhere warning that entry was forbidden by law. But church members broke the locks and forced open the doors, and then they stepped back in awe as they saw row after row of boxes of Russian Bibles stacked from the floor all the way to the ceiling. One husky young man offered to help get the boxes of Bibles down and carry them back to the city even though he'd grown up during another era and wasn't a believer. He disappeared inside the storehouse and was gone so long that people began to wonder what had happened. Finally he reappeared in the doorway triumphantly holding a huge Russian Bible high over his head. Tears filled his eyes as he opened it and pointed to the name inside. "This was my grandmother's Bible," he said as he reclaimed his Christian roots. Things began to change throughout that entire area as believers rediscovered who they were and resumed their ministry as the people of God.

My prayer is that God shall help Christians today to rediscover their true identity as a chosen race, a royal priesthood, the people of God and to resume their ministry to proclaim the mighty acts of him who called them out of darkness into his marvelous light. Selah!

Chapter 4

The Two Ways

One day a minister browsing through the famous Holy Sepulcher library in Istanbul, Turkey noticed something over behind the stacks, and calling for a ladder, he retrieved a handful of parchment papers that turned out to be one of the most important finds in Christian history. They were from a first-century document called the *Didache* (διδαχη), a handbook the early Christians had used as a guide to Christian living. Tantalizing fragments of that document had been found from time to time in church ruins across the Roman Empire. But this was the first complete copy to appear after the book had been lost for over fifteen hundred years. Officially titled *Teaching of the Twelve Apostles* (διδαχη των σωδεκα αποστολων), its discovery in 1673 was an exciting moment for theologians and Bible scholars alike the world over.

The *Didache* begins with a description of the two ways of life similar to those found in Psalms, Job and in other biblical and extra-biblical writings: the way of the righteous and the way of the wicked. "There are two ways," the book says, "One of life and one of death, and there is a great difference between the two." What follows is a set of ethical guidelines that cover virtually every aspect of the Christian life. The handbook even gives instructions on how to conduct church ordinances and contains an order of worship that provides a rare glimpse at life in the early church. No one knows where the book came from, who wrote it, or anything about its origin. However, fragments found in church ruins across ancient Rome give evidence that early Christians used it right along with the Bible itself.

First Peter resembles that early church handbook with an important section on practical morality that comprises the main part of the epistle. Just as Diaspora believers needed a crisis theology worth dying for, they needed a crisis morality by which to live as Christians in a non-Christian world.

First, the epistle deals with the basic principle of honor. "Conduct yourselves honorably among the Gentiles," it says, "So that, though they malign you as evildoers, they may see your honorable deeds and glorify God when he comes to judge" (2:12). After watching fine American GI's take a moral holiday when they came to Japan for R & R during the Viet Nam and Korean wars, this verse in 1 Peter has special meaning to me. The word honorable used not once but twice in the epistle, is from the Greek word that means good. It says Christians are to be good, not just for their own sake but as a witness to those who misunderstand and persecute them. Could such an attitude of honor be partly responsible for the respect and the freedom Christians were eventually granted in Rome?

Honor is an especially important concept in the Orient just as it was to the ancient world of 1 Peter. Several years ago the Chinese ministry of education invited a delegation of Japanese college & university administrators to China for an official visit and I was one of those chosen to go. (I was the only Caucasian in the group.) In addition to arranging tours of universities and colleges across China, the Chinese officials held a banquet for us at the government headquarters in Beijing. But for me, the highlight of the visit was a tour of the imperial palace. We entered from the Tiananmen Square side and almost immediately passed a classroom full of desks. The guide was about to pass by without comment but I stopped him and asked for an explanation of that room. He told us what I already knew, that it was where Confucius had tested prospective politicians to determine if they were qualified to hold government office. The great philosopher believed that people who aspired to rule his nation ought to meet certain basic academic and moral standards. Not a bad idea! Those who passed the test were awarded the title shi, the word for gentleman that designated them as persons of honor. It is still a title respected across China and Japan. In fact, the test for that title was the origin of difficult entrance exams that characterize the educational systems in both China and Japan today.

Next, the epistle has a section on social relationships (2:13–3:22) that is almost identical to the passages on morality in Ephesians (5:22–6:9) and Colossians (3:18-4). For one thing, 1 Peter calls for a radical new approach to domestic relations emphasizing a mutual respect between husband and wife almost unheard of in that day. Paul even expands on the initial relationship between husband and wife in his letter, to include one between parent & child. Naturally, one has to place these instructions in the context of first-century mores to understand their true meaning. Although a woman's role in society then was different from what it is now, it's important to note that her value as an individual was the same as that of a man.

Our Japanese women love this passage in 1 Peter because it is primarily about a believer's relationship with a non-Christian spouse. It's very difficult for Japanese church members to find Christian marriage partners and they struggle with the issue of family life when the spouse is a non-Christian. Although 1 Peter doesn't forbid marriages to non-Christians, the epistle does call for a patient Christian witness and a prayer for family unity in such a marriage, "So that they may be won over without a word by a spouses' conduct, when they see the purity and reverence of your lives" (3:1-2; Eph 5:22-33). Significantly, the passage on domestic relations closes with a call for the husband to honor his wife and recognize her as a joint heir to the kingdom of God (3:7).

Next, the epistle calls for a new approach to work relationships. That is what the section on slaves and slave masters is all about. Most Christians then were among the sixty million slaves who did most of the work in ancient Rome. Consequently, slave and slave master relationships in those days were the equivalent of relationships between labor and management today.

Slavery is an offensive term anytime, anywhere. It is especially repulsive to those who lived through America's civil rights struggle or to Baptists who cringe at the history of a denomination begun in support of the right to own slaves. But the New Testament passages on slavery have to be interpreted in the context of first-century labor management relationships. Otherwise, a literalistic interpretation of the passage on slaves and slave masters in 1 Peter could easily lead to support for class discrimination, or even worse, to an outright endorsement of slavery. The dynamic theory of biblical interpretation is about getting beyond the literal wording of such passages to understand the deeper gospel truths they hold.

Japanese businessmen often say the United States is a democratic nation politically, but hasten to add that economically it is totalitarian to the core. That is, they say that business decisions in America are made from the top down, where company CEOs draw enormous salaries to control everyone and everything in an organization. Japanese business, on the other hand, is administered by a principle called consensus management, which calls for decisions to be made from the bottom up, where employees and employers work together to reach a consensus. It is a decision process that begins at the lowest level and is passed up the line. The administrator's task in such a system is to coordinate and implement what is sent to him rather than to issue directives of his own. Naturally, the success of such a system depends on good relations between labor and management. Ironically, it is very close to the Christian work ethic that made American business the envy of the world in earlier years.

First Peter also calls for new civic relations: a new attitude of respect towards government. The epistle says that although Christians may be aliens & strangers, they must never become traitors. The writer even calls on Christians to: "Honor the Emperor." But notice the qualifier in that passage. It admonishes believers to "accept the authority of every human institution, for the Lord's sake" (Rom 13:1-7). That's good advice for any age, don't you think?

First Peter reaches a high point as the writer cites Christ's suffering as an example of how believers are to negotiate these difficult relationships: "Christ also suffered for you, leaving you an example that you should follow in his steps"(2:21). Thomas à Kempis's famous novel, *The Imitation of Christ*, written in the fourteenth century and translated into more languages than any other book except the Bible, was based on this passage. And Charles Sheldon's famous novel, *In His Steps* (updated edition by Whitaker House, 2004), put that story into modern terminology that left us with the burning question, "What would Jesus do?"

The epistle lists five essential virtues needed to make these relationships work (3:8). First is the principle of *harmony* that calls for a unity of thought that makes believers alert to the needs of others. The next principle *sympathy* means that Christians are to empathize with those around them: "Rejoice with those who rejoice, weep with those who weep." Again, the principle of *mutual affection* is about love that says to, "Earnestly love one another from the heart." Then, what about *compassion*? This word is derived from the Greek root term for intestines just as the Japanese character for emotions comes from the word *hara* for stomach in that language. It makes compassion a part of one's physical makeup, one's feeling. These days our emotions are so dulled by violence that we often find it difficult to feel true compassion. Maybe you have heard the new term *compassion fatigue* that describes such a feeling. Finally, 1 Peter's emphasis on *humility* seems out of place in an age like ours when self-esteem is the new buzzword. But are not the believers who are willing to accept their limitations usually those who accomplish the truly great things in life? The writer of 1 Peter certainly thought so.

First Peter's closing passage, emphasizing that love is that which ties together such moral teaching, is characteristic of the ethical and moral teaching found throughout God's word. Listen: "*Above all maintain constant love for one another.*" It is reminiscent of how Paul introduced his famous love chapter in 1 Corinthians, "I will show you a more excellent way" (1 Cor 12:31).

One year Seinan University asked me to teach a course on Christian ethics for college seniors, explaining that the fourth year students needed something to prepare them for transition from college to the real world. I was excited about the course and set out to find a text to use but was disappointed to discover that no two books on Christian Ethics treated the subject alike. Normally there are certain basic principles for teaching subjects like math, literature, science and even languages. But ethics was different. Scholars disagreed on virtually every principle for such a course. Finally, I decided that rather than use a text someone else had written I would design my own course. And that is exactly what I did. After defining ethics, I dealt with the theoretical and practical aspects of Christian living and concluded that love was the motivation to draw it all together.

In his monumental work on Christian ethics, Søren Kierkegaard captured the dilemma of faith and action with the Old Testament account of Abraham, poised to sacrifice his son. Kierkegaard was so intrigued with how the great patriarch got beyond custom and tradition in an age that condoned both animal and human sacrifice, that his entire book was spent repeating that same scene over and over again. He told it from every conceivable angle, trying to analyze what happened. Surprisingly, Kierkegaard's main question wasn't how Abraham could possibly kill his boy. That was a given for the age in which he lived, a supreme act of worship. What Kierkegaard really wanted to know was: *what made him stop?* Kierkegaard concluded that this great man of faith spared the life of his son because he reached beyond custom and tradition in a wonderful *leap of faith*.

First Peter tells us that is precisely what believers have to do in every age. Christian ethics is about getting beyond custom, tradition, social mores and living according to the divine principles of love and faith; anytime, anywhere—always!

Chapter 5

The Blood of Martyrs

Tertullian's famous remark, "The blood of martyrs is the seed of the church," captures the meaning of Christian suffering for all ages. The son of a Roman government official in North Africa, this great second century man of God was so impressed by the courage of Christian martyrs that he converted to their faith and became one of history's foremost theologians.

The epistle of 1 Peter is about suffering from beginning to end. But the author surprises us, saying, "Rejoice in your suffering"(1:6). Writing to believers who had experienced the loss of country, home, family, and had endured all kinds of violent persecutions, he even repeats that paradox in the epistle's final chapter (4:13). What on earth could he possibly mean by those words, "Rejoice in your suffering?"

The church's first great test came from without when it was buffeted by wave after wave of persecutions that lasted more than three hundred years. Amazingly, the first wave was that of religious persecutions when Jewish authorities launched a series of attacks against the Christians in Palestine. The book of Acts records in great detail how the Sanhedrin acted to counter what they termed a Christian threat against Judaism. Chapter 4 describes the arrest of Peter and John; chapter 5 records the apostles imprisonment, chapter 7 reports the stoning of Stephen; chapter 8 notes the dispersion of early Christians; chapter 9 relates how Saul, a Roman soldier, persecuted Christians and chapter 12 tells about the martyrdom of James, the head of the Jerusalem church.

Following this wave of religious persecutions, Tacitus, the Roman historian, describes how emperor Nero began a second wave of state persecutions against Christians, accusing them of starting the fire that destroyed Rome. The next emperor Domitianus (90 CE) extended persecutions to the provinces, issuing a government decree that required all Roman citizens to affiliate with a recognized religious body. Christianity was not an option then because it was designated as an illegal religion (*religio illicita*). Believers unaffiliated with a state religion were considered suspect and were arrested—the exile of apostle John to Patmos belongs to this period. The third wave of persecutions (98–117 CE) came during emperor Trajanus's reign when the persecution of Christians became official government policy. A Roman historian named Pliny describes how the decree then stated that Christians were to be offered three opportunities to recant before they were executed—Ignatius was martyred during this period. Christian persecutions became less severe during the next wave (117–138 CE) but even then state religious festivals often became occasions of mob rule when the Romans would suddenly turn against Christians and torture them publicly. Pius (138–161 CE), the next emperor, reinstated the imperial policy of persecuting Christians and made them more violent than ever.

The martyrdom of Polycarp, recorded in great detail by an early Christian historian, provides a rare glimpse at what happened during those persecutions:

> As Polycarp entered the stadium, a voice came to him from heaven saying, "Be strong, and play the man." The proconsul then inquired if he was really the famous Christian they said he was. And on his confessing that he was, the proconsul tried to persuade him to a denial, saying, "Swear the oath and I will release you; revile the Christ." But Polycarp answered, "Fourscore and six years [eighty-six years] have I been his servant and he has done me no wrong. How then can I blaspheme my king who saved me?" Then placing his hands behind him and being bound to the stake, like a noble ram out of a great flock for an offering, a burnt sacrifice made ready and acceptable to God, looking up to heaven he said, "Oh Lord God almighty, —I bless you that you have granted me this day and hour,

that I might receive a portion among the number of martyrs in the cup of Christ unto resurrection of eternal life.—May I be received among these in your presence this day as a rich and acceptable sacrifice. For this I bless you, I glorify you through the eternal and heavenly High-Priest, Jesus Christ, your beloved son, through whom with him and the Holy Spirit be glory both now and for ages to come. Amen." When he had offered up the Amen and finished his prayer, the firemen lighted the fire. And a mighty flame flashing forth, we to whom it was given to see, saw a marvel, yea and we were preserved that we might relate to the rest what happened.[1]

The next emperor, Marcus Aurelius (162–180 CE), was more tolerant towards Christians but even he introduced a spy network to seek out believers he could punish. Justin Martyr was one of those who were thrown to wild beasts during his reign. Emperor Serverus (193–211 CE), who followed Aurelius, reinstated the policy of Christian persecutions and extended them all the way to North Africa where the first great Christian seminaries were located. Classes there had to be moved constantly to protect the students. After another brief period of tolerance under Maximus, the following emperor Decius (249–352 CE) reinstated the policy of violence against Christians. However he provided exemptions for those who were financially able to purchase their freedom. Emperor Valerianus (253–260 CE), who followed next, exhibited a friendly attitude towards Christians at first but eventually yielded to the hardliners, once more resorting to violence.

The last wave of persecutions, under emperor Diocletianus (284–305 CE), was the cruelest ever. Following a period of moderation, he issued a series of edicts that came as a real shock to believers everywhere. The new edict forbade public assembly, called for the destruction of churches and ordered the arrest of all believers. Bibles were banned and there were public book burnings of Christian literature throughout the empire. Eusebius, the historian, reports that Roman prisons were so crowded with Christians in those days there was no room for the real criminals.

But if you're looking for a reason Christians had to suffer then, or why we must suffer now, you won't find it in 1 or 2 Peter. That question was one sounded throughout the Old Testament as writers from Job to the psalmists asked why the righteous had to suffer. But the writers of Scripture discovered that there are no ready, easy, simple answers to the problem of why the righteous have to suffer. We too want answers to that question because we have to suffer for our faith—in one way or another today.

Fortunately, God's word leaves the matter of righteous suffering a mystery. And I, for one, believe it is better that way. To know the depths of life's mysteries would put us on a level with the divine. Faith is the trust that puts eternity into perspective and leaves life's final outcome to God.

I'll never forget walking down the famous Appian Way in a suburb of Rome, Italy, where it is said that Peter met his Lord. That way is not a public highway but a quiet lonely path in the outskirts of the city. My wife and daughter were too exhausted from sightseeing to join me, but suddenly, as I walked there alone, I imagined the apostle Peter appeared there beside me. Together we met Jesus returning to the city and, just as legend has it, Peter asked the Lord that famous question, "*Quo vadis?*" (Where are you going?). Jesus replied, "I'm going back to Rome to be crucified again." You can imagine what happened then, can't you? Peter turned about face and headed back into the city with Jesus, saying, "Wait Lord, I'm going with you." With that, the apostle went back to Rome where he died for his faith. Legend has it that in compliance with his own request, Peter was crucified upside down declaring that he was unworthy to die in the same manner as his Lord.

But take note! The epistle of 1 Peter does something far better than give a simplistic reason for our suffering. It tells us that true believers can find joy even in the pain they endure for their faith. And therein is the paradox that accounts for Christianity's survival during those dark and dangerous years of persecution.

In fact, nowhere in the past have Christians been stronger or happier than when they suffered and died for what they believed. Instead of destroying the church, the persecutions actually made it grow stronger. First Peter tells us why, "Do not be surprised at the fiery ordeal that is taking place among you, but rejoice insofar as you are sharing Christ's sufferings" (4:12). Here, the writer not only prepares believers for the fiery ordeal of persecutions, but tells them to be happy about it because participation in Christ's suffering enables them to share his glory. Furthermore, the truth of that paradox echoes throughout history to challenge us today.

For one thing, the paradox proclaims that the cross and crown go together! The cross is a universal symbol of the Christian faith that tells us that the gospel is worthy of one's ultimate sacrifice. Even the ordinance of baptism symbolizes that the death and resurrection are one. There is no crown without a cross, and no resurrection to the new without death to the old. They go together!

Again, the paradox of pain and joy accounts for the happiness early Christians found in musty catacombs underneath the city of Rome. I saw, with my own eyes, the word for joy written on the walls of those underground caverns. Could it be that the believers who resided there read 1 Peter's admonition, "Rejoice insofar as you are sharing Christ's sufferings so that you may also be glad and shout for joy when his glory is revealed" (4:13)?

Further, the paradox of insult and blessing says that even an insult can become a blessing for the true believer. Or, as the epistle puts it, "If you are reviled for the name of Christ, you are blessed" (4:14). That's because to be called a Christian, even in derision, identifies one with the Lord. And finally 1 Peter points to the paradox of suffering and glory: "If any of you suffer as a Christian do not consider it a disgrace, but glorify God because you bear his name"(4:16). Significantly, throughout the epistle, the word glory is used fourteen times in connection with suffering.

Finally, 1 Peter ends with a declaration of victory, "After you have suffered for a little while, the God of all grace, who has called you to his eternal glory in Christ, will himself restore, support, strengthen and establish you. To him be the power for ever and ever. Amen" (5:10).

Waves of persecution against the church not only failed to destroy it but ignited a faith so strong that Christianity grew more powerful by the day. Even the government of Rome could see that. And with the Edict of Milan in the 313 CE, Emperor Constantine granted religious freedom to believers across the empire.

A Faith that Sings

Japanese people love the story of their nation's famous twenty-six Christian martyrs who suffered and died for their faith. It happened during the years Christianity was banned across that country. There were signs posted everywhere warning that Christianity was an illegal religion, punishable by death. These twenty-six believers were convicted of professing the illegal faith in Kyoto and were sent four hundred miles south to be executed in the port city of Nagasaki. Some say they left footprints of blood in the snow as they marched across Japan's Southern Alps in the dead of winter. Once they reached the city of Nagasaki, twenty-six crosses awaited them on a bill overlooking the Japan Sea. And there they suffered and died for what they believed. Today a huge bronze monument stands on the spot where they were executed and school children across Japan count the twenty-six martyrs among their country's national heroes as they study about their bravery.

While I was chancellor at the university in Fukuoka I used to travel to Nagasaki periodically so I could go to the memorial for those twenty six martyrs in order to mediate and rethink my own stance as a Christian. It is an imposing structure with twenty-six life-size figures of those who died. Meticulously researching each of the martyrs, the sculptor depicted them as farmers, carpenters, businessmen, ministers; even two small boys. And looking up at those twenty-six, I would wonder what went through their minds as they died for their faith.

Then one day I saw something I'd never seen before—an inscription across the top of the monument. At first I couldn't make out the meaning because the words were written neither in Japanese nor in English. They were written in Latin. I knew a few words here and there but I just couldn't put it all together. Finally, one day I called the caretaker and asked if he knew what the inscription said. Proudly, he explained that it was a verse from a well-known Christian hymn. "You mean they were singing when they died?" I asked. He said, "Yes, the twenty-six martyrs were singing out of joy for the privilege of dying for their faith."

Think of it! Theirs was a faith that sang! Their death underscored 1 Peter's paradox about the joy of suffering. Furthermore, their sacrifice gave birth to the vibrant church in Japan today that is living proof the blood of martyrs is, indeed, "the seed of the church." Could it be that such a spirit of sacrifice is what's missing from our own faith today?

Note

1. Henry Bettenson, ed., *Documents of the Christian Church*, 2nd ed. (New York: Oxford University Press, 1967) 10–11.

Chapter 6

Sound Doctrine

Have you made a will? If not, you should! One needs to make certain those things he or she values are passed on to the next generation. That means leaving to one's successors not only the material assets accumulated over the years, but also a person's ideals and values that can help shape their future.

The epistle of 2 Peter is written as a last will and testament, expressed as the apostle Peter's final instructions to his followers. Listen to his own words: "I think it right to refresh your memory since I know that my death will come soon" (1:12). Bible scholars compare this passage in 2 Peter to Jacob's last words to his sons or Moses' farewell address to the Israelites; even to Jesus' final words, at the Last Supper.

Amazingly, the writer's last testament is a warning about the dangers that lurk within the church itself. Believers, at that time, were fighting on two fronts: against external persecutions on the one hand and against internal gospel perversions on the other. Second Peter is about the latter. The Greek word *aireseis*, that the epistle uses to describe that danger, is where our English word heresy comes from. It is pronounced the same way and has a similar meaning. In other words the letter is a warning against heresy.

The main problem with heresy is not that it is the opposite of truth but the perversion of truth. Unlike an outright falsehood, heresy contains elements of truth that make its error much more difficult to detect. In other words, it perverts or twists the truth to make it fit whatever one wants to say. Second Peter explains that such gospel perversions can destroy a church fellowship unless they are combated with sound doctrine.

This warning comes as a shock to postmodern believers who are unaccustomed to dealing with the dangers that confront Christianity from within. They say that our gospel is one of love. And that is certainly true. Love was the central theme of my missions ministry all during an adult lifetime in Japan and it has to be the primary message of our church anytime; anywhere. But make no mistake about it; the dangers of gospel perversions are real and Christians must deal with them today just as they did in the first century, lest the gospel become nebulous and the church irrelevant and meaningless to people of the twenty-first century.

Writing well into the second century, the author of 2 Peter issues a severe warning against false teachers and false prophets who were bringing heretical sects into the church. The opening statement in chapter 2 makes that clear with this passage, "But false prophets also arose among the people, just as there will be false teachers among you, who will secretly bring in destructive heresy"(2:1).

Seminary students are required to study the heretical movements that threatened the church through history because they represent the kind of gospel perversions that can occur in any age. Consider the following heresies the church had to deal with in the first century.

First, there were religious perversions that sought to accommodate the gospel to other faiths. The Nazarenes were an example of that as they attempted to adapt Christianity to Judaism. Although they claimed to be Christians, they held firmly to Jewish legalism and accepted the gospel of Matthew as the only legitimate New Testament book. Eusebius, the early church historian, characterized them perfectly as he wrote, "While they want to be Jews as well as Christians they are really neither Jews nor Christians."

Today syncretism poses the same threat of religious borrowing that, taken to the extreme, risks losing one's spiritual identity. Polytheistic religions find it easier to borrow from monotheistic faiths than visa versa because, logically, monotheism is unable to adopt polytheisms' basic premise without sacrificing its own reason for being.

Secondly, philosophical perversions threaten to turn the gospel of *revelation* into one of *reason*. That was precisely the danger of Gnosticism's attempt to combine Christianity with Greek philosophy.

Its emphasis on human knowledge as opposed to divine revelation hit at the very heart of the gospel of faith. Early church fathers saw that and harshly criticized Gnosticism as outright heresy. Iraenaeus' monumental work, *Adversus Haereses*, was a stinging critique of the Gnostic error, calling the early church back to a gospel centered in faith rather than reason.

Nowadays the New Age movement closely resembles ancient Gnosticism and makes great use of its extra-biblical literature. Bookstores across Atlanta abound with Gnostic literature in their New Age sections. Such literature includes the Gospel of Thomas, the Gospel of Peter, the Gospel of Mary, Acts of Peter, Acts of Phillip and others. There are almost as many volumes of these as there are orthodox Christian volumes in today's bookstores.

The early church also fought against the spiritual perversions found in early Holy Spirit movements. Many scholars attribute to these the beginning of modem Charismatic and Pentecostal churches. Montanism was a case in point. It was begun by a man named Montanos (170 CE) who declared himself the paraclete mentioned in John's gospel and sought to prepare his followers for the second coming. He predicted that event would take place at Phrygia, the site of the New Jerusalem and at first the movement was centered in that area. But by the fourth century it had spread all the way to North Africa where Tertullianus, one of the church fathers who lived in Carthage, became its most famous convert. He wrote that: "The church will indeed forgive sins, but only the Spirit can do this through Spirit filled people and not the church."

Present-day Glossolalia or tongues-speaking movements are examples of the Holy Spirit teaching taken to excess. They cite the Pentecost phenomenon in Acts chapter 2 as Scriptural authority for their actions. However they overlook Paul's warning in 1 Corinthians 14 against the indiscriminate practice of tongues speaking, calling it a language, "Intelligible only to oneself."

Finally, the misuse of Scripture is another form of gospel perversion. One such movement was Marcionism, which rejected the Old Testament on the grounds that its God was unworthy of the Christian faith. Marcion, the founder, was a wealthy sea captain who began his own church in Rome around 130 CE. He soon gained a large following by pointing out differences between the God of the Old Testament and the God of the New Testament. According to Marcion, the Old Testament God created an evil world and cared only for Israel. He called its harsh legalism unacceptable to the Christian faith. But he said the New Testament God was different, hidden at first but eventually revealed as Savior, Redeemer and Lord. Ironically, it was Marcion's attempt to form his own private canon of Scripture that caused the orthodox church to begin work on what eventually became the official New Testament canon.

Unfortunately, Marcion's bible was nothing more than a collection of proof texts. Consequently, it is a good example of how the proof text approach to biblical interpretation can twist and pervert Scripture to make it to say whatever a person wishes it to say.

Now turn back to 2 Peter 1 for the writer's advice about how to withstand gospel perversions in any age. Like the rungs of a ladder, the writer lists the points of sound doctrine that can prepare believers to meet such attacks and hold true to the gospel at all times, "Support your faith with goodness, and goodness with knowledge, and knowledge with self-control, and self-control with endurance, and endurance with godliness, and godliness with mutual affection, and mutual affection with love (1:5-9). When I left Japan, my church in Fukuoka gave me a plaque with this passage written on it in Japanese and I have it hanging over my desk at home as a constant reminder of the way to stay spiritually fit.

Is heresy still a threat to the church today? The free and open nature of our church fellowship is a real blessing. However, it can also be an invitation to disaster! I cringe every time we admit new members without a meaningful vote and recall what Indonesian Christians told me happened to their churches. I was in Indonesia for their National Baptist Convention, spending a couple of weeks on the seminary campus in Semarang. While I was there, a group of pastors described how a subversive political group had entered the Baptist churches in that country for political rather than spiritual reasons. They were radicals looking for an organization to use in their plan to overthrow the government. One by one they'd become church members, professing the Christian faith, accepting baptism and participating in the Lord's Supper just like other new church members. However, their motives were anything but spiritual. It was all part of their devious plan to use the church for political reasons Fortunately, the plot was discovered before it materialized and the culprits were arrested and put in prison. Unfortunately, according to the Indonesian pastors, Baptist churches there still suffer from the stain of that debacle.

In Japan it is customary for new members to stand before church congregations and confess their faith publicly before they are baptized. Normally they do this by reading a statement of their Christian experience during the Sunday morning worship service. It is always the most moving part of any service. I still have the Japanese manuscript one twelve year old boy read before I baptized him at the Okubo church in downtown Tokyo. He told of seeing our church steeple from the pedestrian bridge that crossed a busy Tokyo thoroughfare nearby and described how he made his way through back alleys to the church. He explained how belief in the Christian faith that he found there had changed his life and asked to be baptized. A few years ago when I was back at that church for a revival, this young man attended the meeting each night I spoke, sitting right on the front row with his wife and two children. Afterward he told of becoming a successful research scientist but of continuing an active church life of worship and witness.

Have you heard what happened when Leonardo Da Vinci finished his painting of the Last Supper? It's said that he called in his trusted disciple, showed him the painting and then waited anxiously for his reaction. After hesitating for what seemed like an eternity, the student finally pointed to the chalice, the cup, commenting on its different hues of color and marveling at its beauty. But Leonardo was not pleased. Deeply disappointed that the cup was all this young man could see in the scene he had struggled so diligently to capture, the great artiest shouted at the top of his voice, "The face, the face; look at the face!" Leonardo had not painted that picture for the cup. He painted it to portray Jesus as Lord, to depict his sacrificial life and death and all that it meant to the Christian faith.

This epistle of 2 Peter reminds one how easy it is to miss the central truth of the gospel and focus on the wrong things.

Chapter 7

Tragedy & Triumph in Job

Anyone beginning a serious study of Job should prepare to enter a world of thought that is entirely different from anything yet encountered. First of all, Job belongs to the Wisdom Literature section of the Old Testament, which reaches deeper than most people are accustomed to going in an effort to understand life's problems.

I had a similar experience trying to understand the reasoning process in the Orient because it was unlike anything I had encountered in the West. But one day a grand old Japanese gentleman named Zenda Watanabe described the difference between Western and Oriental thought as the difference between suitcase logic and *furoshiki* logic. He said Western logic is suitcase logic where everything has to fit together perfectly like things do in a suitcase. "Oriental logic is just the opposite," he said, "it is *furoshiki* logic where the package is made to fit the contents." A *furoshiki* is a small piece of Japanese silk cloth about the size of a woman's scarf that is used to hold books and other objects that one wishes to carry. Normally people lay the *furoshiki* cloth on a table and place their things on it. Then they wrap the cloth around the items and tie it together. If there are just a few things to carry the package can be made small, or if there are a number of items the package can be made larger. Our Japanese believers used to tie their Bibles and songbooks together with a *furoshiki* and bring them to church, often traveling long distances on commuter trains.

The book of Job tells one the answers to life's complexities aren't always in neatly arranged patterns that point to obvious conclusions and calls the reader to reach deep in order to understand life's true meaning. Scholars cite Job as the literary high point of all Scripture because it explores the mysteries of evil and suffering that have plagued humankind from the beginning of time and does so with the elegance of poetry, dialogue and drama that, without offering a simplistic solution to life's most complex issues, reveals yet another profound realm of divine truth.

What is so unique about Job that we should study his life, or about his story that it deserves a place in the sacred Scriptures? Obviously he is no famous general who led his troops to a military victory. Nor is he a hero, in the usual sense of the word that people look up to with admiration and praise. Quite the opposite! Job is the central character in one of the darkest and most depressing books of all time. But it is precisely the questions that his misfortunes, his suffering and the dark side of his life raise, that have resonated with people throughout history and brought new faith and insight to those who struggled with similar issues.

To put it simply, Job is universally loved because the book is about what happens when life falls apart at the seams. Who among us has not suffered some life-threatening adversity and cried out in despair, "Why?" Not only does the book of Job deal with the issue of suffering per se, it's about the more complex problem of why the righteous have to suffer. Ultimately it is about the meaning of life itself.

Overview

At the outset, a brief overview of Job is essential to establish the book's origin and nature and to understand its message. First, *who* wrote the book? Rather than a single author it is evident that numerous writers contributed to the story. However, scholars generally agree that an unknown genius of an editor drew it all together into a complete whole. *When* was it written? Although the story of Job is an ancient legend, the book's actual date of writing is rather late, clearly postexilic, (circa 500–300 BCE). Apparently it was written to put the tragedy of Babylonian captivity into perspective. *What* is unique about its literary style? The prologue and epilogue are in prose and frame the magnificent poetry that makes up the main body of the story. Originally the poetic section was chanted and even nowadays is best understood when it is read out loud. *Where* does the book of Job fit in Scripture? It belongs to a division of Scripture known as Wisdom Literature but deals with the complex issue of righteous suffering that is found throughout the Old Testament. "Why must the righteous suffer," is the question asked repeatedly throughout Psalms, Proverbs and from the beginning to the end of the book of Job. *Why* was Job written? The book of Job was written to address the complex problem of suffering, specifically that of righteous suffering.

The fact that Job's story is Gentile rather than Jewish distinguishes it from other Old Testament literature and gives the book a universal flavor right from the start. There were persistent folk tales from across the entire Middle East about a *good* man who lost everything and was subjected to the same kind of suffering that Job experienced. Among these were stories of a Sumerian Job (1750 BCE), a Mesopotamian Job (1000–700 BCE), and an Egyptian Job (1800 BCE). The Old Testament account of Job was a story first passed orally from generation to generation before it was finally put into writing. The book's main characters are Gentiles rather than Jews including Job. Elihu is the exception because he is a Jew. The central portion of the book that is written in poetry also uses Gentile names for the divine. The name for Israel's God, YHWH, appears primarily in the prologue and epilogue—it is used there twenty three times. But elsewhere Job uses Gentile names for the divine: El Shaddai, Adonai Eloah—this is a name for God found nowhere else in Scripture. Finally, the story of Job has a Gentile setting, located in the land of Uz (Edom?), east of the Jordan River.

All this means that the book has a universal message for all people as it wrestles with one of life's most perplexing questions: why do the righteous suffer?

Job's answer to the complex issue of righteous suffering, as I see it, is given in four stages. First, the book's prologue depicts Job's misfortune as a form of testing intended to reveal the extent of his faith. Second, Job's three friends misinterpret his suffering as retribution or punishment for past sins, the traditional explanation given for suffering in those days. Third, Job's own speech is a subjective approach to the problem, searching for a more intimate fellowship with the Lord. And finally, the writer of Job reaches deep in an effort to understand suffering as a means of divine revelation. Of course, the progression of these four answers is what counts, and in the study that follows we shall explore each of these stages in greater detail as we contemplate the breathtaking truths they hold.

Two pivotal passages in Job capture the book's contrast of tragedy and triumph. First is the tragic cry of desperation in chapter 7, where Job begs the Lord twice just to leave him alone, "I loath my life—I would not live forever" he says, "Let me alone!" Or again, "Will you not look away from me for a while, let me alone until I swallow my spittle?" (7:16-19) Is not this the same cry of desperation that all of us have raised to God at times, saying, "Oh Lord God, please just leave me alone!" The Japanese word picture for suffering, *kunan*, is a compound of two Chinese characters: one, the word picture for intense pain and the other, a character that shows a flock of blackbirds swarming on a tree. This character depicts suffering as a series of small events that snowball to completely overwhelm a person. It is like sibling pestering or school bullying, that suddenly reaches the point when one cannot stand it any longer and cries out, "That's enough, leave me alone."

The second pivotal passage in Job is one of triumph which Handel, the great composer claimed for his musical masterpiece, *The Messiah*. Can't you hear those words from Job now as choruses around the world join to sing triumphantly, "I know that my redeemer liveth?" The King James Version of the Bible that Handel uses for that quotation may be a bit stilted for our day. But if anything, the NRS rendition of Job 19 is even more powerful: "I know that my Redeemer lives, and that at the last he will stand upon the earth; and after my skin has been thus destroyed, then in my flesh I shall see God"(19:25).

Understand this is the pre-Christian concept of a redeemer. Here, the word *redeemer* is not the Greek term λυτρω, which the New Testament uses for Christ's redemptive work but the Hebrew word *go-el* that means someone who testifies to another's integrity. Technically, it's the legal term for a close of kin who has the right to buy or redeem a relative who has been taken into slavery or to recover a plot of family property. The Old Testament uses it repeatedly to describe how God redeemed the Israelites from Egyptian slavery and from Babylonian exile. The word redeemer is used eloquently in the nineteenth Psalm and elsewhere throughout the Old Testament. One could even speculate that Jesus had Job's words in mind when he said, "I am the resurrection and the life" (John 11:25).

I'm convinced that this scene of triumph in Job is precisely what Handel's *Messiah* makes it out to be. On the one hand, Job's life was clouded, not only with suffering and misfortune, but also with the prevailing doctrine of divine justice that attributed Job's pain to retribution. From beginning to end the book reflects a prevailing sense of despair. But the passage about redemption in 19:25-27 is one of those magical moments when Job envisions not only a new meaning to divine justice, but a new understanding of the nature of the divine. Just imagine how Job must have felt when he saw, maybe for the first time, God as his redeemer.

Finally, one has to turn the story over and look on the other side to see its paradox: that the faithful often discover life's true meaning once they lose everything else. Hope isn't easy to come by in the book of Job. It lies deeper in the soul of God's word than most people are prepared to go. But it's there nonetheless, and those who find it are rewarded with a profound new understanding of life's meaning that changes them forever.

I'm reminded of the story that an elderly minister told of his boyhood days in Nova Scotia. He said he lived where the tide would sometimes ebb as far as two miles out and on occasions when it was out the farthest, he and his pals would play on the fresh sands and climb the rocks that were left in its wake. The eagles built their nests on those rocks and it became great fun for the boys to climb up and steal their eggs. But one day instead of eggs, he and his buddies found a nest of baby eagles and as mischievous boys do, they took one of the birds home with them. Not knowing what to do with the little eagle they put it in the pen with the baby chicks. Amazingly, the baby bird grew quickly but in the process completely lost its eagle consciousness and was seemingly content just to be like the surrounding chickens.

Occasionally it would spread its wings but never once did it attempt to fly because the chickens there were unable to do so. Then, one clear day as the young bird stood in the chicken yard gazing into the heavens, another stately eagle flew majestically overhead. Slowly the young eagle spread its wings full length and after pausing to look around one last time, with a firm flap of those strong wings, flew off into blue to soar the heavens as it was created to do. What happened? The eagle had caught a glimpse of its true nature and that changed its life forever.

Instead of giving simplistic answers to the troubling questions of life's reverses, Job takes believers to a divine level of faith for a transcendent view of life's ultimate meaning and assures them that God is in control; always!

Chapter 8

The Question

Hiroshima was not just another city in Japan to my wife and me; it was one of our strongest Baptist centers and after the atomic carnage there, the deaths, mangled bodies and radiation sores of our own church members made Job's tale of righteous suffering come alive in an unforgettable way. Unlike Nagasaki, the other atomic bomb site that was surrounded by a protective mountain range, the city of Hiroshima was on a level plane with nothing to shield its people from the terrible radiation waves that inflicted havoc on everyone and everything in their path. We saw in Hiroshima the same kind of innocent suffering that had occurred in Poland's Holocaust death camps—or later at New York's twin towers—and we knew that the question heard throughout the Old Testament was one that is still with us today: Why, oh why, must the righteous suffer?

The book of Job holds a number of answers to Job's probing question of why the righteous suffer but the first answer appears right at the outset of the story. The prologue reads like a novel as it explains that Job's suffering is a life test proposed by Satan, designed to measure the extent of his devotion to God. According to the story, Satan taunted the Lord to just try Job and see if he doesn't "curse you to your face."

Incredibly, the New Testament tells us that Jesus himself experienced a similar test. Matthew 4 is like a page out of Job as it records how "Jesus was led up by the Spirit into the wilderness to be tempted by the devil." The writer of that gospel goes on to explain that Jesus underwent three days of testing designed to prepare him for his public ministry. The great Russian author Dostoyevsky was so impressed with the passage in Matthew that when he was asked which page he would choose if he could keep only one page from the Bible, he said he would want the one from Matthew four because it was where Jesus identified with our humanity and demonstrated how to handle adversity. Our students at Seinan University in Japan used to tell us that our entrance exams were something inspired by the devil. The school had such a good reputation that each year over twenty thousand young people would take the entrance exams to compete for a mere six hundred sixty coveted vacancies. That meant we had to make the tests rather difficult in order to yield the number of students that our university could accommodate. Since one of my jobs as a professor there was to monitor those entrance exams I can still remember what a painful experience it was to walk up and down the isles and watch teenagers, just out of high school, struggle with questions that most adults in America could not answer correctly. Beyond that, I had to continue testing those who later signed up for my classes.

But guess what? After graduation from the university many of those same students would come back to thank me for the kind of painful testing that helped them grow intellectually and spiritually. Some continue to do so even now.

Job 1 retells the story and gives a brief summary of the meaning as the author draws it all together with these famous words, "The Lord gave, the Lord took; blessed be the name of the Lord!" (1:21)

First Job said, "The Lord gave." Today, we would use the word blessed to describe Job as one who was extremely well blessed. He was blessed with a fine family; he was blessed with good health; and he was blessed with possessions in abundance. If anyone could sing the gospel song we used to love to sing at church as children, he could: "Count your many blessings, name them one by one." Surely Job was one who could rejoice as he looked back over his life, and sing with gusto, "Count your many blessings, *see what the Lord had done.*"

Scholars cite parallels between the perfect beginnings in the Genesis Garden of Eden and what happened in Job's garden of Uz. The six scenes that begin the story of Job are similar to the six days in the creation story. Even the recurrent numbers of seven and three that are used to describe Job's initial state indicate perfection just as the garden of Eden was perfect. They remind one of the primary numbers that Japanese artists use to achieve symmetry and beauty in such things as Ikebana (flower arranging) and other Oriental art forms. As a rule, one would never make a Japanese flower arrangement using even numbers such as two, four, six, eight, etc. because these are the weaker numerals that can be divided. The stronger numbers are those that cannot be divided: one, three, five, seven, and nine. They're the primary numbers that stand for perfection. Interestingly, the latter numbers are those used in Job's prologue to identify his family, his livestock and his possessions. They tell the reader that Job's life initially was perfect and complete in every way.

Then something happened to spoil Job's perfect world and he said, "The Lord took." He spoke of the dark night of testing that happened without warning as messengers came in rapid succession reporting Job's loses, leaving the book's hero with virtually nothing. Gone were his possessions, his family, his health and all of those things he held dear. Worst of all, his suffering and misfortune occurred despite Job's deep faith. The writer made it clear right from the start that Job was "a blameless and upright man who feared God and turned away from evil."

Here again, one sees a parallel between Job's troubles and those in the garden of Eden. Neither book uses the word devil to identify the spoiler because there was as yet no frilly developed concept of a devil. Instead, Job calls him the adversary or Satan.

But notice that Job clearly designates YHWH as the one who took. There is no hint here of a Persian dualistic battle between good and evil. Nor is it a Gnostic attempt to rationalize two separate good and evil deities. The book of Job makes it clear throughout that God controls all things, including the forces of evil. This is evident even in the book's final chapter where the Lord's speech identifies the two land and sea monsters, Behemoth and Leviathan, as God's creations and proclaims them beings under his governance. My favorite English poet, William Blake, even interpreted Satan in the book as Job's own doubts. But to dwell on the issue of Satan in this passage is to miss the point of the story: Job's ultimate test of suffering and how he dealt with it.

Georgia Harkness, a former Vanderbilt University professor, quotes St. John of the Cross in her magnificent book *Dark Night of the Soul* (Abingdon Press, 1955), as she calls what happened to Job his dark night of the suffering. In modern terms the story of Job is about severely tested church members who are just as unsure how to handle their pain today as was Job long ago. A fine Christian young lady in Japan was so overwhelmed by her problems that she came to me asking how to become a nun. I told her that it was not unusual to want to escape from life's problems and many devout Christians try to do just that. But I explained that her problems were apt to follow her into a monastery and told her that ultimately the way to handle such difficulties was not escape but confrontation.

Finally, Job's soliloquy has a wonderful surprise ending: "Blessed be the name of the Lord." Although it is true that the Hebrew word to bless can also be translated to curse, this expression in Job is a well-known Hebraic benediction that leaves little doubt the word blessed in this passage is intended as an expression of praise and thanksgiving.

The Japanese language has two words for testing: *shiren* and *kunren. Shiren*, the first, is the sort of testing intended to hurt someone. But *kunren*, the second, is the kind of painful testing that causes one to grow and become a better person. Job's testing was the latter. His suffering was that which left him with nothing tangible but gave him an inner faith and understanding that was far more valuable. No wonder Job lifted his hands heavenward in thanksgiving and praise saying, "The Lord gave; the Lord took; blessed be the name of the Lord."

I'm reminded of the way the famous music composer, Saint-Saens, captured the joy and pain of learning with his beautiful symphony for children: *Carnaval des Animaux*. Midway through that music one hears a familiar melody played in grand style by two pianists using two pianos. At first the music sounds familiar but one simply cannot remember the name of the tune. Then suddenly he or she recognizes it as the practice scales that novices use when they're learning to play a musical instrument. The symphony, that is, is a parody on the pain and joy of learning. For me, those scales still bring unpleasant memories of the endless hours that my mother made me practice the piano while neighborhood kids played baseball just outside of our living room window. I hated those hours I had to spend in practice back then. But today, although I am an extremely poor pianist, I wouldn't trade anything for the music appreciation I gained. Do you suppose Job had something like that in mind when he shouted, "Blessed be the name of the Lord?" It's like my university students in Japan who still come back to thank me for the painful testing they endured during their college years. "Thank you, thank you," they say "for helping me to mature." Isn't that what Job was saying to God?

I was serving as pastor of the Yokohama Baptist Church in Japan when a distraught young mother came to me for counseling on one occasion. Her daughter had been told that she passed the entrance exam for the city's premier high school and was all set to enter that school the next semester. But at the last minute she was abruptly refused admission. Upon hearing what happened, her friends chided her saying, "Your family's no good," "It's the result of something bad in your life." They were words that hurt to the core and the girl rushed home to her parents with tear-stained eyes and outstretched hands. "Is it true?" she wanted to know. "Are my sins really being punished before all the world?" Her father was an important government official for the area and it was a question that cut to the core for the entire family. When the telegram came saying that this girl had been refused entrance to the elite high school, the deadline was already passed for applications to other inferior schools and the family rushed to ask school officials for reconsideration. But no amount of reasoning would work and the parents were forced to leave in anger and discouragement.

The mother came to me in tears asking what she could possibly say to console her daughter. I pointed to Paul's words in the Romans 8: "We know that all things work together for good for those who love God." Then I explained that God's word assures us that our suffering is not necessarily punishment for our sins. I told her that bad things happen to the righteous and the unrighteous alike but the right question to ask at such times may not be "why" at all. That's something only God can answer. Instead, we should ask how God wants us to use the experience to grow stronger. Suddenly the young mother's eyes brightened, and she rushed home to tell her daughter that her school problem wasn't punishment for her sins but to encourage her to find practical ways to use that experience to grow spiritually and intellectually and to become a better person.

Job's first answer to the question of why the righteous suffer, is that God's testing causes believers to grow stronger when they cling to their faith as the gospel song "O Jesus I Have Promised" says, to the end.

Chapter 9

Divine Justice

One of the first things you'll run into in the Orient is the Hindu doctrine of *karma* or it's Japanese equivalent, *inga or mukui*. In Japan I heard the word *mukui* used so often in everything from daily conversations to academic discussions that I was terribly curious to know what it meant. But I was totally unprepared for its complexity upon learning that the English translation for *mukui* is retribution. Just imagine using the English word retribution on the playground at school or during a coffee break at the office.

The Oriental concept of reward and punishment maintains that whatever happens is both the result of a person's past and determines his or her future. Taken to the extreme it depicts an endless lifecycle of cause and effect that characterizes a religion of fate. Not surprisingly, Gautama (Buddha) sought and achieved an escape from that vicious cycle with his famous breakthrough called enlightenment, an intense form of meditation that enabled him to rise above it all to a nebulous state called nirvana.

Job's second answer to the question of righteous suffering came at approximately the same time in the West that Gautama wrestled with the same problem in the East. This answer is found in Job's debate with his three friends concerning the meaning of suffering. After discussing the cause of Job's misfortune at great length, his three comforters all ended up saying the same thing: that Job's suffering was a form of retribution, or punishment for past sins. They accused him of some terrible wrongdoing that brought on the suffering and called on him to repent.

Job's outburst of anger at such a charge actually began the debate that covers the main portion of the book. He cried out demanding to know why he was born into such a fate. Then a series of why questions followed that wreaked with agony at his plight: "Why did I not die at birth?" (11, 12); "Why was I not buried'?" (13-19); "Why is light given to one who cannot see the way?" (20-26). A continuation of his complaints follows in chapter 7 as Job replies to Elihaz's first speech, "You scare me with dreams and terrify me with visions" (7:14). Further, he agonized out loud saying, "Let me alone." Satan's claim that the Lord had "put a fence around him" to protect Job was no longer valid. The world had suddenly come crashing down on him and his family (1:9). Any wonder that he wanted to know why!

That is when Job's friends came to offer comfort. The great Baptist theologian G. Campbell Morgan once wrote, "I like these guys," explaining that they did all the right things for such an occasion. They "wept aloud, tore their robes, and threw dust on their heads"—all customary expressions of concern and grief for one in those days. Further, the way they sat with him seven days and nights in silence is precisely how Dr. Wayne Oats, my pastoral counseling professor at Southern Seminary, taught students to comfort people as ministers. But for Job things deteriorated rapidly and all three friends ended up accusing him of some terrible sin that brought about his great suffering and misfortune.

The debate that follows centers on the cause of Job's misfortune. It consists of three rounds during which the three friends contend that his suffering was retribution for past sins. Job straightway responded, denying the charge and defending his integrity.

The first round of the debate is about divine justice (4:1–14:22). Here, Job's three comforters take turns defending what they believed to be the justice of God. *Mispat*, the Hebrew word for justice, is a concept crucial to an understanding of the Old Testament. Originally it meant that God was partial to the righteous. In their opening arguments Elipaz, Bildad, and Zopher all three eloquently presented the traditional retribution theory of justice that questioned Job's righteousness. Elipaz's rhetorical question is especially intriguing, "Who that was innocent ever perished?" (4:7-11). Or "Can mortals be righteous before God?" (4:17). He argued that Job should accept his punishment like a man. Then Bildad followed with his cause and effect metaphor of two plants, comparing the fate of Job's children to what happens to papyrus and reed plants that have no water (8:11-15).

Job doesn't buy it. His answer, found in chapters 9 and 10, is an imaginary trial of the divine. What transpires as Job, a mere mortal, pits himself against an omniscient God is painful to watch. The outcome that is assured from the beginning reminds one of Franz Kafka's masterwork, *The Trial*, in which the protagonist is arrested, accused, tried, and executed without ever learning the reason. Job's trial, like the one in Kafka's novel, is a vivid description of humankind's pitiful plight before society's warped understanding of divine justice.

In the second round of the debate the fate of the wicked is at issue (15:1–21:34). Elipaz and the two others attempt to refute Job's observation that the wicked actually do prosper at times. They call Job's position, that cites the affluence of evil people, an affront to divine justice and immediately jump to God's defense, insisting that the wicked have to be punished.

Job refuses to accept that line of reasoning too. Sure, the wicked must be punished but not always in this world, he contends. Then he turns the tables on his accusers, questioning their stance as instructors to an almighty God. "Will any teach God knowledge, seeing that he judges those that are on high," Job asks. Further, he observes that "One dies in full prosperity, being wholly at ease and secure, his loins full of milk, and the marrow of his bones moist. Another dies in bitterness of soul never having tasted good. They lie down alike in the dust, and worms cover them" (22-26).

I'm reminded of a famous play by the dramatist Rostand about a rooster named Chanticleer who thought the sun rose every morning because of his crowing. Sure enough, when this rooster crowed each morning the sun actually did rise, like clockwork. But one morning he forgot to crow and the sun rose that day just as always. Suddenly Chanticleer realized that his crowing had absolutely nothing whatever to do with the sunrise. But instead of shrinking in despair, he made this tremendous observation, "It may not be my poor voice which brings on the day, but there is something I can do and nothing can deprive me of the joy of it. If I cannot cause the sun to rise, I can at least lift up my voice to celebrate the dawn." That's precisely what Job is saying in the debate. Although he recognizes that the wicked and the righteous share many of the same rewards in this life, he chooses to worship the transcendent Lord.

The third and final round of the debate is where Job's accusers take one last shot at him. Having failed to convince Job of his transgressions with conventional wisdom, his so-called friends did what people always do in such a situation they began a character assassination against him (22:1–27:23). Chapter 22 of the book lists Job's sins one after another, even recounting, among other things, his unjust treatment of others "for no reason" (22:1-11). Clearly his accuser knew all Job's weaknesses and ruthlessly accused him of wrongdoing.

But Job knew better. Were not these the very same things the accusers themselves had done at times? He knew his own deep love for God and how he diligently sought the Lord, even when it seemed the divine was hiding from him. I like the way the word integrity that the book uses here to describe Job's character is the same word that appears in the book's introductory chapter. It maintains that Job remained a person of integrity even when he lashed out against God. Although Job lost everything else, there was one thing he knew he could not afford to lose no matter what. He simply had to hold firmly to his integrity as a believer, as a person, as a man of God. Doesn't that say something important to Christians today?

Job's accusers used a form of theological reasoning known as theodicy that attempts to vindicate divine justice by allowing evil to exist. But then, aren't we all guilty of the same thing, accusing others in order to defend God; as if we could! That line of reasoning came very close to a belief in the fate that characterized numerous other religions that surrounded Israel. Concerning fate, I always remember a scene from my favorite movie, *Laurence of Arabia*. Everyone thought Laurence had lost his mind as he set out in a sandstorm to find one of his men who had been lost in the desert. "It is his fate to be lost and die, leave him alone," they said. But when Laurence returned carrying the wounded man on his shoulder, he looked squarely at his critics and said, "Fate is what you make it."

The book of Job clearly rejects retribution as the reason for righteous suffering and calls on believers to look for the real answer, not in outworn traditionalism but in a renewed relationship with their Lord.

I'm reminded of one experience we had during our missionary careers coming to America on furlough. A highlight of those furloughs was always a trip to the Rock Eagle assembly grounds just off I-20 for missionary retreats and seminars. We would go there practically every time we came to the states and speak to thousands of young people from across the southeast to study about missions. It was an indescribable thrill to touch the spirit of tomorrow's leaders on those occasions.

But I was always curious to know why they named that place Rock Eagle. I could find nothing anywhere to suggest that eagles once lived there. But one day I noticed a pile of rocks at the entranceway and climbed the tower that stood nearby. When I reached the top and looked down at the rocks below, guess what I saw? From below those rocks had appeared like any ordinary pile of stones, but when seen from above they formed the perfect shape of an eagle in flight. From atop the tower it was clear that someone had arranged the rocks that way on purpose. As I contemplated the way ancient Indian workmen had followed instructions to build what they could not see, I remembered God's directions that we too are to build on faith.

Job's story assures us that not only does God have a design for our lives; he will show us how to perfect it as we follow his instructions even when we cannot see what we're building.

Chapter 10

Signs of Recovery

In his novel titled *Chinmoku* or *Silence* (published 1966), a Japanese novelist named Shusaku Endo lashed out at God for abandoning Christians in Japan during World War II. The author is a Japanese Christian who grew up during bombing raids that rained fire on over thirty million people where he lived in greater Tokyo. The book asks why God remained silent while so many people suffered across the land he loved. It is now a classic, acclaimed for the veiled answer it gives to that nagging question of innocent suffering. It answers its own question with the profound observation that God wasn't silent at all—but spoke loudly and clearly through everything that happened during those years of turmoil.

Job also felt abandoned by God as he questioned the Lord's silence before his own suffering. "Oh that I had one to hear me," he agonized in his final speech in chapter 31. On another occasion, he cried out, "Why do you hide your face and count me as your enemy?" (13:24). Again, Job struggled for intimacy with the divine saying, "Oh that I knew where I might find him" (23:3). One recalls that Jesus expressed similar feelings of loneliness as he cried out from the cross, "My God, my God, why have you forsaken me?" (Mark 15:34). But then, haven't we all felt abandoned by God at one time or another?

Job's healing began as he turned inward in search of the reason for his suffering. His faith had survived the severest kinds of physical and psychological testing and he had withstood those terrible accusations of retribution from friends and religious professionals. But now he turned to the more difficult task of getting beyond his own doubts through a closer relationship with the divine.

A famous quote from the book of James in older translations that alludes to Job's patience is both a mistranslation and a misnomer. The passage used to read: "You have heard of the patience of Job, and you have seen the purpose of the Lord, how the Lord is compassionate and merciful" (Jas 5:11 KJV). However, Job was anything but patient as he adamantly defended his innocence. In newer versions of Scripture, the word "endurance" (την υπομονην) is used rather than "patience" as the more appropriate translation. Paradoxically, it was Job's very struggle with the Lord that led him to find the intimacy he sought.

Job's speech in chapters 29–31 reads like a series of steps necessary to the kind of healing he sought. He tells of moving progressively towards recovery as he reaches deeper and deeper to examine his inner spirit.

Ironically, the very hurt and anger to which earlier chapters alluded were Job's very first steps toward healing. Paradoxically Job's awful wish that he had never been born was an essential part of his recovery. The Israelite faith is credited with having a place for such anger towards God in its religious language because to deny such a natural reaction to adversity is to postpone or even prevent recovery.

Next, Job's journey of healing continued with an expression of gratitude for past blessings. The entire chapter 29 is devoted to reminiscing about the good times Job and his family enjoyed with God before things took a terrible turn for the worst. "By his light I walked through darkness," he wrote, remembering the Lord's guidance during those difficult years of pain and suffering. Again, in a truly beautiful passage of gratitude for family Job wrote, "The friendship of God was upon my tent." He gave thanks to God for physical blessings saying: "The rock poured out for me streams of (olive) oil" (4-6). Then, remembering the good reputation he enjoyed in the marketplace, Job wrote: "They listened to me and waited and kept silent for my counsel" (21-23). He also thanked God for the numerous opportunities to minister to the needy: "I was father to the needy and I championed the cause of the stranger"(15-16). Finally, Job gave thanks for the personal virtues God had granted, "I put on righteousness, and my justice was like a robe and a turban" (14). These wonderful memories were all important steps to Job's recovery.

I too know something about the healing power of good memories. One Christmas night in Japan I was so angry with God that I could hardly pray because my wife had just been diagnosed with bone cancer and we had to drop everything and return to America. Not only did her illness and death end our missionary careers, I am still finding sketches of pictures she planned to paint, outlines of books she intended to write, and notes of poems she meant to compose during retirement. I was upset at God for taking her at such a crucial moment in both our lives! But after her death I was able to heal when I turned from the pain of losing her and began to recount the blessings we'd shared during our years together as missionaries in Japan. Those memories enabled me to move on to the work the Lord still had for me to do.

Another step towards Job's healing was reverse-truth awareness similar to Paul's assertion that his very weakness was his greatest strength. Remember how the apostle began that famous passage in 2 Corinthians enumerating the dangers he'd encountered: "frequent journeys in danger from rivers, danger from bandits, danger from my own people, danger from Gentiles, danger in the city, danger in the wilderness, danger at sea, danger from false brothers and sisters; in toil and hardship, through many a sleepless night, hungry and thirsty, often without food, cold and naked." He then concluded, "If I must boast, I will boast in the things that show my weakness" (11:25-30). But that's when Paul heard the Lord say, "My grace is sufficient for you; my power is made perfect in weakness" (12:9). Job learned the same lesson, that one's very weakness often becomes the occasion for an outpouring of divine strength.

At last Job was able to heal as he accepted responsibility for who he was. It happened with his confession of sin. In chapter 31 he enumerates a succession of sins that cover virtually every misconduct imaginable. Lois captured that stance in her poem called "An Amulet":

> She wore my prayer,
> an amulet upon her troubled heart.
> And for a moment fear was cowed
> and faith came to impart

> A quiet peace, a healing strength,
> a hope that pain would end.
> But prayer to her was just a rite.
> She called no god her friend

After listing his sins in great detail, Job ends with an astonishing document called an oath of innocence. It's where he declares: "I'm innocent of everything on that list" (31:37). According to civil law then an oath of innocence absolved one from any wrongdoing and put the burden of proof on the accuser. He even offers to sign the confession to make it official. "Here is my signature," he says, agreeing to place his seal on the imaginary document. The Hebrew word for signature was the last letter of the Hebrew alphabet, the letter taw. Since it is written like the English letter X it is undoubtedly where the present day custom originated for using an X when someone is unable to sign his or her own name. Interestingly, the same thing is true in Japan where one's personal signature is not acceptable to make things legal. People there have to carry a registered seal called a *han* to use for official documents. Job's offer to finalize his oath of innocence with an X indicates that Israel had the same custom.

If the steps to Job's healing sound like a description of the how Christians must heal today, they should. I'm convinced that the same struggle that brought Job to a more intimate relationship with the Lord can lead people out of depression and sorrow again today. Anger at the situation, gratitude for past blessings and a confession of innocence are all means of communicating with the divine. And just as these steps enabled Job to emerge from his suffering stronger than ever, they can help people heal again today. This same relationship between pain and growth was important to the survival of people of faith throughout Japanese Christian history. During the two hundred years that Japan was closed to the West there were signs posted everywhere across the country warning people that the Christian faith was forbidden under the penalty of death. In those days the authorities used a *fumie* test to determine who the offenders were. The word *Fumie* is written with a compound Japanese character composed of the symbol for a picture and another for the verb to step on. Literally it was a step-on-picture that officials used to identify those suspected of being Christian. Officials would place a picture of Christ on the floor and order people to step on it. Those who refused were immediately accused and severely punished for being members of the forbidden faith. However, amazingly, the number of Christians grew steadily in spite of such persecution and today Christianity is exploding across Japan in a way that's nothing short of miraculous. A recent religious survey (March 17, 2006) of Japan by the Gallup Poll organization showed that the number of Christians grew from one half of one percent of the country's population after the war to six percent of the total population today. Further, the survey shows that Christians make up 12 percent of those who profess any faith at all. In addition, it reveals that the number of young people claiming the Christian faith is now at an all-time high.

Ultimately God did speak to Job through his very suffering in a way that has inspired and challenged readers throughout history.

When I was chancellor at Seinan University, I invited a Christian judge of Japan's Supreme Court to be the feature speaker for our religious focus week one year. There was so much excitement on our campus when he agreed to come, that we began to fear our chapel would not hold the crowd. Finally, I asked members of my staff to hang loud speakers along the eves of the chapel so people could stand outside and listen as he spoke. And that year the campus was literally covered as people came by the thousands to hear this great man of God.

I'll never forget how the Judge began his message that first day. He walked over to the podium and opened his Bible to the first chapter in John's gospel. Then he stepped back and began quoting all eighteen verses of the prologue from memory. He quoted not in Japanese or English, but from the original Greek text that began—(Εν αρχη ην ο λογος)—"In the beginning was the word and the word was with God and the word was God." Then when he finished, the grand old Japanese gentleman walked back to the podium and, holding his Bible high overhead, looked squarely at out students and said, "This is where my life began fifty years ago when I was a college student just your age, in a chapel just like this." He then told how God had guided him through one difficult life crises after another and concluded with a challenge for our students to establish secure spiritual foundations on which to build their careers, their homes and their future lives.

Job's recovery from an experience of innocent suffering teaches us that the same steps of anger, gratitude and confession are essential to one's spiritual healing in any age.

Chapter 11

The Final Answer

Dr. Paul Tillich, an all time theological great, used to tell his students at Harvard University to look for the divine in the depths of cultural beauty: art, literature and music. He urged them to seek the Lord's presence in unusual places, areas outside the normal parameters that people set for God in their lives. Japanese people use this same spirit to characterize their culture as the art of the unspoken, the unpainted and the unwritten where what is not there is often far more important than what is.

The whirlwind in which God spoke to Job doesn't seem strange at all when one considers the unusual ways that God communicated with his people elsewhere in the Old Testament. Remember how he addressed Moses from the burning bush or guided the Israelites by a fiery cloud in the wilderness? Even God's crucial message to Elijah 'was via a wonderful still small voice. And if I read Job right, he would have us believe that God continues to address us in magical new ways again today.

Suspense builds as the book of Job reaches a surprise ending when YHWH lifts his servant Job to a divine realm and answers him from a whirlwind. At last, it was God's turn to speak. But instead of giving a direct answer to the problem of suffering, the Lord's reply was something far more important. Actually, there are few direct answers in God's Word to questions that people ask about the divine. Remember Jesus' reply to the crucial question, "Are you the one to come or shall we wait for another?" He said, "Go and tell John what you see and hear," an answer similar to the one the Lord gave Job centuries earlier, (Matt. 11:3-4).

Like Columbus who set out to find a new route to India but discovered a whole new world instead, Job sought answers to his moral difficulties but gained a whole new perspective of divinity and humanity; of life, death and eternity.

The speeches of YHWH found in Job's final chapters are far more than direct answers to the problems of humankind. They are revelations that trace the transcendent power and presence of the divine all the way back to creation. Not only do the speeches offer assurance that God is creator, they also proclaim him as Lord. Furthermore, the final YHWH messages are profound affirmations of the Judeo-Christian monotheistic distinctiveness.

The first whirlwind speech makes it clear that God is creator and as such is the rightful questioner concerning matters of this life. Heretofore Job was the questioner, at one point conducting an imaginary trial of the divine in an effort to discern the reason for his suffering. In his book *When Bad Things Happen to Good People*, Harold Kushner gives a forceful translation of the way the divine responded to Job's inquiries with a cross examination of his own:

> Where were you when I planned the earth? Tell me if you are wise. Do you know who took its dimensions, measuring its length with a cord? Were you there when I stopped the sea and set its boundaries, saying, 'Here you may come but not further?' Have you seen where the snow is stored, or visited the storehouse of the hail? —Do you tell the antelope when to calve? Do you give the horse his strength? Do you show the hawk how to fly?[1]

Constant references to creation in Job have caused many scholars to see parallels in the book to the Genesis account of creation. They compare and contrast events in the garden of Uz and in the garden of Eden. Together the two Scriptures attest to the greatness and power of God as the creator and source of all life.

Compared with the Judeo Christian concept of the divine, the Japanese word for a god, *kami* is an extremely weak term. During the forty-three years we were in Japan, there was always a huge sign hanging across the front of the Central Railway Station in downtown

Tokyo that read: *Yorozu no kami no kuni* ("This is a country of ten thousand gods"). The Japanese word *yorozu* (lit., "ten thousand") really means "too many to count." It's something like the root "pan" in pantheism. The Japanese concept of innumerable deities means that Christians across Japan and the Orient struggle for ways to express the biblical concept of monotheism. Fortunately, our Japanese Christians solve that problem by using the term Creator God, or *Tsukurinushi naru kami*. It sets the Christian God apart as the ultimate authority for all of life. Job's powerful revelation of the divine as creator assures believers that he understands their problems and is able to heal their pain. At times, God's word even reverses the order of creation from life to death to death to life in order to show that either way God is in control.

The second whirlwind speech asserts that the divine also manages his creation as Lord. "Have you an arm like God?" he asked. "Can you thunder with a voice like His? —tread down the wicked where they stand, bury them in the dust together?" Here, the Scripture cites Behemoth and Leviathan as the two land and sea villains that represent the dark side of creation. Behemoth resembles the hippopotamus and Leviathan is a beast that relates to the crocodile. Ultimately it is a speech that proclaims God even controls the forces of evil.

In one sense of the word, Job's whirlwind speeches are answers to theology's perennial debate about which is more crucial to our knowledge of God, reason or revelation. Even today theologians line up on both sides of that issue. But Job's dynamic depiction of life as a mystery only God understands is ample evidence that revelation is the only legitimate answer to that question.

Finally, the story ends with Job's recommitment to the Lord in a whirlwind experience of faith. At first, his response to the divine in chapter 42 is somewhat of a disappointment. True, it acknowledges God's authority as Creator and Lord. But if anything, its tone is anticlimactic, ambiguous and even a bit subdued, compared to Job's colorful speeches elsewhere in the book.

Suddenly, that all changes as one realizes there's something much more profound in this passage. I made that discovery while reading the English translation of Job's final speech in the *Jewish Study Bible*:

"Indeed, I spoke without understanding of things beyond me, which I did not know—I had heard you with my ears, but now I see You with my eyes." I discovered that Job was describing nothing less than a whirlwind experience of divine revelation, an experience that transformed his life forever.

Job's analogy of a whirlwind reminds me of how Akaiwa (a respected Japanese theologian) compared the conversion experience to an earthquake. A person can find refuge in a storm cellar during a hurricane's swirling winds, but when the ground moves beneath one's feet, there's absolutely nowhere to go to escape an earthquake's fury. It shakes buildings and basements alike; trees and earth move as one; and houses and cellars crumble together. "That's what happens in conversion," Akaiwa says, "It affects every aspect of people's lives. It changes them socially, ethically, spiritually and remakes them into complete new persons."

One of history's most famous conversions came to light in connection with a traffic accident in Paris, France. Auto accidents are common in contemporary America, but in seventeenth-century Paris an unidentified man was run over and killed—not by an automobile, but by a horse-drawn carriage. At first the victim was unidentified, but when doctors examined the body, they found a document sewn into the coat lining that identified him as Blaise Pascal, the renowned scientist. The document they found was not about science at all; it was an account of Pascal's conversion to the Christian faith. Pascal was so moved by what happened when he became a Christian, in the year 1634, that he recorded it and sewed copies of that account into each of his garments. He said he wanted to have a record of his conversion next to his heart at all times as a constant reminder of the new relationship he had with his Lord.[2]

This final scene in Job is like that. When Lois and I were crossing the Pacific aboard an ocean liner from San Francisco to Tokyo, there was nothing ahead but water as far as one could see. There were no markers to indicate whether we were traveling on the right course. But from the rear of the ship the view was altogether different. There, one could see that the ship's wake had parted the waters leaving an unmistakable path all the way back to the horizon. It was clear evidence that we were traveling a straight course toward our destination.

Job reaches deep to depict suffering as a form of God's revelation that lifts the believer to the realm of faith for a life perspective that let's us know God is in control—always!

Notes

1. Harold Kushner, *When Bad Things Happen to Good People* (New York: Avon, 1983) 50.

2. A. J. Krailsheimer, *Conversion* (London: SCM Press, 1980).

Chapter 12

Jeremiah: Prophet to the Nations

Traditionally, people have taken three different approaches to understanding history. First is the progressive view that sees history as a constant upward movement towards a better world. The second, or regressive interpretation of history is just the opposite. It questions whether present day societies are morally and spiritually superior to those of ancient times. A third approach is the classical view of Greek philosophers that understands history as a cyclical movement, neither progressive nor regressive, that at times repeats itself.

Christian historians, however, use the word *geschichte* to describe an event view of history that interprets certain pivotal events as those which transcend the normal chronological order to become focal points around which all else revolves. A good example of this is the way people's lives revolve around such crucial events as graduation, marriage, or the birth of a child.

The book of Jeremiah is like that, an important part of the *heilsgeschichte*, or salvation history, that holds messages not only for the ancient world but for all time.

Prophets were essential to the survival of the Israelites because they lifted people to the level of the divine during periods of great turmoil and gave them a vision of future hope. They painted no rosy picture of conditions back then. They told it like it was. But they inspired God's people to envision what could be, what would be, what future possibilities there were for those who loved God and remained faithful to his calling.

Jeremiah was just such a prophet, one of the most intriguing personalities in all Scripture. He was a committed, courageous, progressive, tragic person, who, pained by the depraved plight of the Israelites, took on government, society, religion, and even other prophets. He challenged established ways of thinking, questioned Israel's status as a chosen race, and called on his nation to repent, but he promised an abundance of divine comfort, guidance, and hope to those who remained faithful to their Lord. Not only did Jeremiah's message of hope speak to the ancient Israelites, his spiritual objectivity challenges believers in every age to step outside the accepted structures of religion and government to hear what God is saying to them.

Our study proposes to place Jeremiah and his message in the proper cultural and historical context in order to glean truths applicable in any age. First, one has to decide whether to organize the material by dates, speakers, or to follow the order given in Scripture. For the purpose of this study I have chosen a spotlight approach, highlighting certain representative passages that capture both the prophet and his message.

First, the role of prophets in ancient Israel was unique in the history of world governments. They were wise men of God, placed outside the normal structures of government and society, who were expected to analyze national issues and call for needed reform.

The Hebrew word for prophet, *nabi*, meant someone called to be God's spokesperson, a person endowed with a divine message. The prophet's task was to deliver God's word, not just to predict future events as a fortuneteller. The prophet's message—translated oracle in the newer versions of Scripture—was originally rendered burden in the King James Version because it wasn't always what people wanted to hear. *Takusen*, the Japanese word for "message," a compound of two Japanese characters, says it best: *taku* for trust and *sen* for message, something entrusted to one by the Almighty.

The seventh century BCE was a time of great turmoil when Judah was tossed like a football from one foreign power to another. During Jeremiah's lifetime the control of his nation passed between three different world powers: Assyria, Egypt, and Babylon. Ultimately that's what brought about Jerusalem's downfall and sent large portions of its citizenry into exile. It was a time when God's people desperately needed someone to put things into perspective and offer them hope for the future. Incidentally, the closing chapters of 2 Kings and 2 Chronicles in the Old Testament record the events of this period in great detail.

Jeremiah was a man with a complex personality. On the one hand he was courageous and progressive, but on the other hand he was deeply melancholy and introspective. In one of the greatest sermons ever, he boldly condemned Israel's outworn religious structures and called for needed reform. But on other occasions, he withdrew from public life for extended periods of depression. A series of laments or confessions in chapters 11–20 records what happened during those latter periods. A famous Japanese theologian named Uchimura unwittingly described Jeremiah when he wrote: "A saint is generally understood to be someone universally loved and respected, but I disagree. A true saint is someone depressed and rejected by the world who, despite what other people think, stands strong for what he believes."

The latter part of the book tells the story of the prophet's tragic life. It records how he was forbidden to marry (16:1), was put in prison numerous times (38:5), and on one occasion was ordered by king Jehoikim not to speak in public. Fortunately he got around the latter by dictating the speeches to his secretary who, in turn, read them for him (36:1ff). On another occasion the king tore up one of Jeremiah's manuscripts and threw it in the trash while he watched. But later the prophet had Baruch rewrite that manuscript for posterity. The book also records how he was ridiculed (18:18), falsely accused of deserting to the Babylonians (37:11 ff), and even once talked of quitting (20:9). However, under Gedaliah Jeremiah experienced a peaceful time that inspired his beautiful dream of future hope, eloquently expressed in the book's section about a new covenant (chs. 30–31). Unfortunately, the prophet died a sad and lonely death in Egypt where he'd been taken against his will (27:7ff).

The book of Jeremiah is absolutely magnificent. However, Carroll, a well-known Old Testament scholar cautions, "The reader who is not confused by reading the book of Jeremiah has not understood it."

That's because it is a collection of different types of materials with no chronological order, at times terribly hard to follow. Some scholars claim that the book is written backwards because it begins with Jeremiah's prophecy (chs. 1–21) and concludes with the story of his life (chs. 26–52).

Generally, the book's content is attributed to the prophet himself but it is clear that Baruch, his secretary, wrote much of its material. Chapter 36 describes how Jeremiah would first deliver his messages orally and then dictate them to Baruch who put them into written form. Dr. James Watts comments that the book of Jeremiah resembles the spontaneous speech of a preacher rather than the finely wrought literature of a writer.

The text itself shifts back and forth between prose and poetry. But while the poetry adds great beauty and depth, it too, at times, is terribly difficult to follow. That's because poetry doesn't translate easily from one language to another. A lovely Japanese haiku poem, for instance, can fall perfectly flat when translated into English. The problem is not just that of language differences but of cultural dissimilarities as well. The same is true of Hebrew poetry. One has to look beyond the poetic expressions to discover their real beauty and meaning. Of course, the book of Jeremiah abounds with picturesque language and metaphors throughout. Note especially those passages on the potter's wheel (ch. 18), the two baskets of figs (ch. 24), and the parable of the yoke (ch. 27).

The translation one uses to study Jeremiah is also important. I discovered the necessity of a good translation while trying to comprehend the thought of the great Danish philosopher Søren Kierkegaard. I was unable to fathom the meaning of his existential philosophy the first time I read his works in English, but after reading a better translation from the Danish original, his ideas became like arrows that pierced my mind with a whole new worldview. For those who are unable to read Jeremiah in the Hebrew text, the newest and best translation is needed to discover the depth and power of his message.

Finally, Jeremiah did something absolutely incredible for the people of his day. He proclaimed a personal religion, a religion of the heart and a religion of hope that could free the Israelites from the outworn structures and meaningless ceremonies of temple worship. Next, he laid the foundation for Babylonian exiles to find new forms that would forever change the way Jews and Christians worshiped. Examples of such iconoclasm can be found in Jeremiah's magnificent temple sermon, in which he tore away one external layer of religion after another, pointing people to the fundamentals of an individual faith and a personal relationship with the divine. Isn't that what Jesus did for the Jews at Nazareth and Luther, Zwingli, and Calvin did for the Protestant Reformation?

Again, the prophet's persistent call for people to repent and return to God is a theme that echoes throughout the book. His contrast of human stubbornness with that of animals is scathing at times (8:7; 18:13-14). Yet his picture of repentant believers standing before God's grace brings tears to the reader's eyes, "Return faithless Israel, says the Lord, I will not look on you in anger, for I am merciful says the Lord" (3:12). Finally, he depicts the divine as a personal God who weeps with his people in moments of sorrow and rejoices with them in times of victory. In other words, Jeremiah's God is one intricately involved in the affairs of humankind.

An example of Jeremiah's dynamic metaphors is his unforgettable image of the Creator in the parable of the potter. What a jewel that is (ch.18)! The story is set in the Hinmon Valley just south of Jerusalem where some of the world's finest pottery was made. Artists there could take a worthless piece of clay and shape it into something of real beauty. But as any artist knows, things do not always turn out as planned when creating a vessel or painting a picture. Sometimes the medium takes a course of its own and the object is ruined in the potter's hand. Often, the problem is that of flawed material or of sand in the clay. Whatever the cause, the artist must decide whether to discard what he started or to reshape it into something better.

The potter in Jeremiah's parable is none other than the Creator Lord. Here, the image of the divine is decidedly different from the autocratic sovereign depicted elsewhere: he is free to reshape his wayward creations into something better. At one point Jeremiah actually says God changes his mind (18:8). What about that? "If that nation, concerning which I have spoken, turns from evil, I will change my mind about the disaster that I intended to bring." Is this a declaration of God's freedom? I think it is! Jeremiah depicts the divine as one free to minister to those who with their own free will return to him in faith.

Is the book of Jeremiah a subtle wake-up call for present day Christians to find powerful new structures that can minister to a new global age? Read Leonard Sweet's *SoulTsunami* (Zondervan, 1999)! It depicts today's churches as those desperately trying just to hold on to what they have. Clearly something is missing; something important! Jeremiah's message is an ageless prophecy that reaches across history with a dynamic vision for our own age.

It reminds me of Kierkegaard's story about installing a new set of lanterns on his horse-drawn carriage. At first he was perfectly fascinated at the way the lamps made it possible for him to travel at night, explaining in great detail how those two lanterns, one on each side of the carriage, moved with the vehicle, lighting the path ahead. But as if stunned at the discovery, he expressed regret that the lights were so bright he could no longer see the stars.

These days our own world is changing so rapidly it is impossible to keep up with all the gadgets that make life easier. Scientists tell us that just around the corner a whole new world of nanotechnology is about to change things even more. *But we must never forget the stars!* Pray for prophets who, like Jeremiah, can point beyond this troubled temporal world to the transcendent message of a Heavenly Lord!

Chapter 13

A Global Mission

Jeremiah's call to become God's prophet came at one of the most thrilling times in world history. In China Lao Tzu was busy proclaiming the Tao, the way of harmony that gave the world Taoism (*Tao* means way in Chinese). In India the Upanishad Scriptures were heralding a dynamic union between the individual soul (the *Atman*) and the universal soul (the *Brahman*) that became the basis for Hinduism. In Persia Zoroaster had just founded the religion of Zoroastrianism that is so very close to Christianity. And just as Jeremiah's ministry was coming to a close in sixth-century Israel, Grautama and Confucius were teaching their doctrines of enlightenment and loyalty in Asia; a new age of Greek philosophy was underway in the West.

It was precisely such a time in Judah when the Lord showed Jeremiah a new world and gave him a global mission. In the same way that Americans are being thrust into a new internationalism today, the Israelites were entering into new and intricate relationships with the nations surrounding them in Jeremiah's day. The new horizons of religion and life confronting God's people then called for a new world-view to transcended the narrow provincialism they'd known previously.

My own world, like Jeremiah's, was much too small when I accepted the call to preach and left Georgia to enroll in the Southern Baptist Seminary in Louisville, Kentucky. After graduation from that school I fully intended to return to my home in Atlanta and find a church nearby to pastor. That was the extent of my world then: the city of Atlanta, the state of Georgia, the Southern Baptist Convention, and the United States of America. Beyond the things I'd grown up with everything else was blurred and out of focus. But then something wonderful happened; during those seminary years the Lord showed me a whole new world, one that changed my life forever. He showed me God's World.

The description of Jeremiah's call in chapter 1 (vv. 4-10) is especially moving. The only reason we have a record of it is that twenty years later the prophet took time to look back and analyze what happened. He even tells us that the first section of the book was written in retrospect.

Jeremiah was a PK, a preacher's kid, born into a proud family of priests that could trace their lineage all the way back to Shiloh (1 Kgs 1:28–2:26). More is known about his early life than that of any other Old Testament prophet. In fact, the book's very first verses tell us that he grew up in the southern kingdom during Manasseh's reign, in a village called Anathoth, just three miles north of Jerusalem. Something happened when Jeremiah was coming of age that set his life course: the book of covenant law was discovered in the temple where it had remained neglected for centuries and young king Josiah began a reform movement that inspired Jeremiah to join him. He even continued striving for those reforms after the king's death.

I can identify with Jeremiah's call to the ministry because, like mine, it wasn't the dramatic earthshaking experience that other biblical greats had related. Compare it with Isaiah's vision of heavenly beings when he was called to prophesy (ch. 6), or with the vision of wheels that accompanied Ezekiel's call (Ezek 1; 2). There was no blinding light in Jeremiah's call like the one that knocked Paul off his horse in Acts 9. Like Jeremiah's, my own call to the ministry was something for which I'd prepared all my life. As a young seminary student I was often intimidated by the earthshaking experiences other students used to describe their calls to preach. But the Lord even told Jeremiah that he was born to be a prophet: "Before I formed you in the womb I knew you and before you were born I consecrated you" (1:5). Furthermore he'd been a regular at Temple ceremonies and as a boy had sat at the feet of Israel's finest priests. Even his name, YHWH hurls, signified a family background of priests. In addition, Jeremiah grew up during the golden age of prophecy surrounded by and profoundly influenced by a host of other prophets.

A biography of missionary Adoniram Judson that I read as a teenager greatly influenced my own call to the ministry. Since that book had a rather flamboyant title, *Splendor of God* (by H. W. Morrow, William Morrow & Co., 1929), I had expected a success story about a missionary who traveled to another country where he preached to thousands and baptized hundreds of new converts. But Judson's story was not that at all. The book was about a lonely missionary who poured out his heart years on end in a foreign land with only a handful of converts to show for it. It was such a depressing account of the difficulties he encountered far from home that I wanted to put the book down and forget about Judson and his troubles. Yet, I simply could not shake the nagging question of why he would continue to minister under such circumstances. Why didn't he just quit and take his family back to his homeland in America where he would find love and respect and where people would respond to his ministry?

Then one day, I understood. I knew why Judson stayed in Burma and why he continued to witness despite the difficulties. He stayed because that was the work to which God had called him. God's call was all he had and God's call was all he needed to sustain him and his family. Jeremiah's call was like that; he prophesied despite the difficulties he faced because that was what God had called him to do.

In addition to God's call and his vision of God's world, Jeremiah was given God's message. The account of how God imparted his message to Jeremiah is deeply moving, "The Lord put out his hand and touched my mouth" (v. 9). It's a beautiful way of saying that in addition to God's call to be his spokesperson, the Lord gave Jeremiah something to say. Another passage puts it this way, "You shall serve as my mouth." I used to remind my seminary students in Japan that the great reformers through history pointed to God's word as the basis for their reforms. Once these men of God saw the church slipping into ritualism, ceremonialism and secularism, they called people to return to the word of God; to God's message.

Next, Jeremiah was given God's mission: "to pluck up and to pull down, to destroy and to overthrow, to build and to plant." The six verbs used to describe his task appear repeatedly throughout the book. Although it was a task that brought constant criticism, pain and loneliness, Jeremiah was always conscious that the mission was not his alone. It was God's mission.

Dr. W. O. Carver, our mission's professor at the seminary, used to tell us that missions was not about our mission or even the mission of the church. He called it the *missio Dei* or the mission of God. He emphasized that it was God's mission in which we participate. Carver continually pointed to that great passage in Ephesians 3 about God's purpose for the church, continually reminding us that the task of missions was far deeper and broader than anything we had imagined.

Jeremiah also recorded two visions that told him his prophecy was in God's timing. The first vision was an almond tree, a tree highly regarded in Palestine because it was the first to blossom in the spring. The Hebrew word for almond, *shaked*, resembles the word for "alert" in that language and symbolizes that God is always alert to the needs of his people. In Japan the plum tree, the *ume*, is regarded in much the same way because it blooms so early, often while there is still snow on the ground. Japanese people say it symbolizes strength. Jeremiah's second vision was that of a boiling pot blowing steam from the north. It signified that trouble was brewing from that direction which spelled danger for the Israelites.

Jeremiah's sense of calling and commitment reminds me of the story Japanese Baptists tell about a pastor in the southern city of Wakamatsu. He was so committed to the gospel ministry that he continued preaching even after he was hit in the eye with a spear. It happened at the close of the nineteenth century as the Wakamatsu congregation was out doing *robo dendo*—holding a street meeting. As was the custom, one of the members strapped on a huge drum and led the congregation through city streets, beating it loudly enough to draw a crowd. When enough people had gathered they would stop and let the pastor preach a sermon. However, since Christianity was still new to Japan, at times they would encounter animosity, and on this occasion someone threw a spear that hit the minister squarely in the eye. Instead of stopping to find a doctor he reached up and pulled the spear out of his eye with one hand, then used the other hand to cover that eye and stop the bleeding. It's said that he then continued preaching with blood streaming down his face, even issuing a call for people to repent and believe the gospel. I've reconfirmed the truth of that story from the current pastor at Wakamatsu Baptist church. I can believe the story because it is characteristic of the type of sacrificial witness early Japanese Christians made as they laid the foundation for an age of gospel ministry in Japan. It's a witness not unlike the one Jeremiah gave centuries ago.

Am I the only one who feels that a strong sense of God's calling and God's mission is missing from American Christianity? We go to great pains to make church as interesting and as entertaining as possible. But the question is whether the pull of God's call, God's message, God's mission, and God's timing is there. (And doesn't it have to be, for our churches to have any meaning at all?) Remember how Paul in his letter to the Corinthians called preaching foolishness. Our Japanese Christians say that passage means what we do in church is nonsense, foolishness, and meaningless unless God's Spirit is there. I'm convinced that Jeremiah's sense of calling and commitment is essential in our twenty-first-century churches today if we are to fulfill the missions task that God has entrusted to his people.

Chapter 14

Broken Marriage Syndrome

When I arrived in Japan in the late forties, people there told me their culture was one where believers related to many different religions rather than exclusively to one faith. They said that most Japanese people were married by Shinto ceremony, were buried by Buddhist rites and lived according to the Confucian code of ethics. I found that to be true during the years that followed. For instance, when a couple was ready to marry in those days, normally they sought out a Shinto priest to perform the ceremony. But over the years things changed and now so many young couples are choosing to have Christian weddings that they are rapidly becoming the norm.

What happened? Why are so many Japanese young people today choosing Christian weddings? Reread the words of the Christian ceremony and you'll understand the reason. They are excited about entering into a covenant relationship with God and with one another as they seek to establish new homes founded on the principles of faith and love.

Jeremiah portrays the Israelites' relationship with God as a marriage gone sour (2-11). In the broken marriage passage in chapter 2, the prophet returns to the image of Judah as a faithless partner so often that it becomes crucial to understanding his prophecy.

Before examining Jeremiah's description of Israel's broken marriage, we need first to establish what is meant by a good marriage. Some may protest that this is something people know already. But not so fast! How many still hold to the biblical concept that marriage is a lifelong commitment, "so long as you both shall live" or still honor the ceremony's closing pronouncement, "What God has joined together, let no one separate" (Mark 10). Even Exodus depicts Israel's covenant relationship with God as that kind of a marriage (Exod 19–24). Jeremiah gets our attention right away as he uses male and female parts of speech to identify Judah and Israel as the two marriage partners in that nation's relationship with God. He uses the feminine word for YHWH's wife, Judah (2:17-25) and the masculine form of speech for YHWH's spouse, Israel (2:4-16). Basically, the former says that the southern kingdom of Judah is no more faithful as a marriage partner than Israel and deserves to suffer the same fate as its northern neighbor. Note Hosea's strong influence on the prophet here, especially the similarity between chapters 1–3 in Hosea and chapters 2–4 in Jeremiah.

But let's not get ahead of the story. Jeremiah chapter 2 begins with a reminder of Israel's former happy relationship with the Lord, "I remember the devotion of your youth, your love as a bride, how you followed me in the wilderness" (2:2). Let's call this period the Israelite's honeymoon years with YHWH.

Do you remember your honeymoon? Lois and I were married at the First Baptist Church in Tokyo just five days after I arrived in Japan. After the ceremony we boarded a train for the Japan Alps and spent our honeymoon week in a log cabin at Nikko's beautiful Lake Chuzenji. It's a serene lake at the top of the world, said to be one of the world's deepest bodies of water, nestled between two of the country's highest mountains. The scenery there is simply breathtaking, and amid the quiet beauty of that place we got to know one another at the deepest level for a love bond that has outlasted death itself.

Israel's relationship with the Lord was like that. It began with a mutual covenant at Mt. Sinai where God promised his people, "If you obey me fully and keep my covenant—you will be for me a kingdom of priests and a holy nation" (Exod 19:5). The covenant was reciprocal and conditional, promising God's blessings in return for his people's faithfulness. That is, it made the Lord's blessings dependent on the nature of Israel's response, a relationship that continued between God and his people through their early days as a chosen nation.

Then something happened that caused God to charge Judah with the worst indiscretion imaginable. "Has a nation changed its gods," the Lord demanded to know (2:11). Not only had Judah been unfaithful, Jeremiah depicted its alienation from YHWH as a condition worse than any of the surrounding nations' disloyalty to their heathen gods (2:10). It was a state of affairs the prophet called absolutely shocking: "Be appalled, O heavens, at this, be shocked, be utterly desolate, says the Lord" (2:12-13). He followed with a metaphor that compared what Israel was doing to substituting stale cistern water for clear pure spring water (2:13).

Notice the additional metaphors that Jeremiah used to depict Israel as a rebellious partner (2:20-29): *oxen*: that broke out of the yoke; *harlot*: who wandered into a degenerate lifestyle; *vine*: a healthy vine that became wild; *stain*: a guilt that would not wash out; camel: an untrained young camel with no sense of direction; *donkey*: an animal in the heat of lust; and *thief*: one who was shamed when caught.

Next, the prophet doesn't mince words as he calls Israel's broken relationship with God a divorce (3:1-5). "If a man divorces his wife and she goes from him and becomes another man's wife, will he return to her? —Would you return to me?" It is a rebuke against Judah for seeking to return to God with no lifestyle change. The prophet even mentions the pitiful plight of the children in such a marriage (22ff).

Unfortunately, divorce is so common in America today that it is difficult to talk about it anymore, even in church. I read statistics recently that reported fifty-seven percent of all marriages in the U.S. end in divorce. True, that figure probably includes repeats, but the number is still appalling. For someone who spent an adult lifetime in Japan where divorce is still most uncommon, it's pretty hard to accept.

The next passage reminds one of what the philosopher Diogenes once did to demonstrate the depraved moral condition in Greece. Remember how he carried a lamp even in the sunlight, diligently searching for something? When people would ask what he was seeking, he'd say he was trying to find an honest person but had yet to find one. It's the same picture Jeremiah draws of the depraved condition in Jerusalem where God dares the Israelites to try and find even one righteous person in all Jerusalem: "Run to and fro through the streets of Jerusalem, look around and take note! Search its squares and see if you can find one person who acts justly and seeks truth" (5:1).

But it would be a mistake to conclude that Jeremiah's prophecy is without hope. God's promise of mercy accompanies a resounding call to repent that is heard throughout the book, "Return, faithless Israel says the Lord. I will not look on you in anger, for I am merciful, says the Lord" (3:1). What a clear indication it is that God never completely deserts his people. It's the wonderful promise that when Israelites return from exile there'll be shepherds to lead them as they rejoice and multiply their numbers.

Notice that the prophet's call to repent uses two of the most profound terms in all Scripture: First is the Hebrew word *sub* that means to turn or return. It says that people have to come back to YHWH the same way that the New Testament Greek word *metanoia*, for repent, says: with a one hundred eighty degree change of heart. The other term is the Hebrew word *hesedh*, translated mercy, in older versions of the Bible. More recent translations render it loving-kindness. The true meaning is somewhere between mercy and love. It's found throughout the Old Testament; but my favorite passage is Psalm 136. This Psalm repeats the word *hesedh* 126 times in a refrain that says, "His mercy endures forever."

Finally, it is important to remember that Jeremiah is not just about what happened in ancient Israel. It's a picture of our own broken relationship with the Lord in the twenty-first century. We don't hear the word sin much anymore in America. And since the Japanese words for sin and crime are the same, ministers there have to be extremely careful not to mistakenly call people criminals when they use the word for sin. But people everywhere understand what a broken relationship means and Jeremiah's vivid description of that condition in relationship to the divine calls people to reexamine their spiritual lives in any age.

Philip Yancey, author and former editor of *The Christian Century*, tells of a life-changing experience that happened during a rebellious time in his life. He'd returned home to help his mother move into a retirement home and as they were going through her things he found a crumpled and soiled picture of a small child. When he asked his mother who it was, she said, "Why son that's you; that's a picture of you when you were small." At that, Yancey asked why on earth she'd kept such a dirty, dilapidated photo of him when she had literally hundreds of good ones. Then she retold the story of how his father had contracted polio and died when Philip was just a child. She said his breathing became so difficult they had to put him in one of those iron cylinders that people used as lung machines for polio patients in those days. His father's head rested on a shelf at one end of the cylinder, and they attached a mirror to it so that he could see and talk to visitors. His mother said his father talked so much about his young son that she took a picture of him and pasted it to that mirror where he could have it before him at all times. Then she told Philip that his father prayed constantly for his young son until the day he died. "That's the picture," she said, "It's special!" Yancey said his rebellion ceased from that moment and his life took a different course as he heard again the story of his father's great love for him.

The book of Jeremiah is a forceful reminder that the joy of a restored relationship with the Lord is the same for believers today that it was for the Israelites of old.

Chapter 15

Temple Sermon

We now turn to one of the most profound messages in the entire Old Testament: Jeremiah's temple sermon. The sermon is an absolute masterpiece as the prophet raises the age-old question of form and content in connection with worship. He speaks not only to issues of religious life in the seventh century BCE, but to the twenty-first century as well as he lashes out against outdated and meaningless forms and calls on believers to find new ways to express the true spiritual content of their faith. While the world around them was changing rapidly, the Israelites were holding tenaciously to stale religious structures and traditions from another age. As one reads Jeremiah's cutting words about the problematic practices of sacrifice and other issues of Jewish worship there is an unmistakable feeling that he is speaking to churches today, attacking things that need to be changed in present day Christendom.

Who knows what went through the prophet's mind as he joined the temple festivities in Jerusalem that day? The smell of sacrifice and incense filled the air as people chanted their ancient confessionals and temple priests were busy blessing it all. But Jeremiah was uncomfortable with what he saw. He felt something terribly important was missing from that scene and decided someone simply had to question the spiritual content of it all. So, with a sermon for the ages, the prophet Jeremiah confronted the issue of temple worship head on.

Westerners who visit Japan's shrines and temples today are amazed to discover how closely they resemble the Old Testament houses of worship. They have the same holy of holies and the alters of sacrifice that remind one of the Jerusalem temple. There are outer courts and inner courts, even pillars of stone like those found in ancient Israel.

Standing on the grounds of a temple in Japan one can imagine what Jeremiah saw and felt as he addressed the crowd of worshipers that day long ago at the temple in Jerusalem.

Notice the abject irony with which Jeremiah began his sermon: "This is the temple of the Lord, the temple of the Lord, the temple of the Lord" (7:4). Is the prophet mocking some liturgical phrase that had lost its meaning? Could this be an attack against the supposition that people can appease God by repeating meaningless phrases and by performing acts of ritual sacrifice? Jeremiah's sermon is a virtual litany of outdated religious structures that needed to go.

First, the prophet shocked temple worshipers that day by attacking the ark of the covenant. He claimed that it had lost its significance and should be removed from Jewish life. Imagine that! Israelites considered the ark one of their most sacred possessions. It's where they kept documents and artifacts from their nation's history: manna from the wilderness wanderings and Aaron's rod that budded. Most importantly, it held the Deuteronomic code, that which people considered a symbol of God's presence. They had carried the ark everywhere they went, dragging it behind them during their desert wanderings and taking it with them into battle to assure military victory. An attack on the ark was considered an attack on everything sacred to the Jewish faith. There was even a central place reserved for the ark in the tabernacle and later in the temples at Shiloh and Jerusalem.

But Jeremiah sensed something ominous about the ark that went beyond mere symbolism. Was it perhaps the danger of idolatry? "Would the ark be missed if it were removed?" he mused. Answering his own question the prophet wrote, "They shall no longer say, "The ark of the covenant of the Lord, it shall not come to mind, or be remembered, or missed; nor shall another one be made" (3:15-18). Evidently, Jeremiah's criticism of the ark was right on target because it wasn't long after the temple sermon that it disappeared altogether from the worship scene in ancient Israel.

Next, the prophet took on temple worship itself. The temple was at the heart of the Jewish faith and had been since the first one was dedicated at Shiloh. Later, Solomon built the beautiful Jerusalem temple as the fulfillment of David's dream. But Jeremiah felt something was terribly wrong with what went on there. Its rituals had become so perfunctory that he sensed God's people were in danger of losing their distinctive faith. Listen to what the prophet said about that: "Here you are, trusting in deceptive words to no avail. Will you steal, murder, commit adultery, swear falsely, make offerings to Baal and go after other gods you have not known and then come and stand before me in this house, which is called by my name and say, 'We are safe!'" (7:7-10). The Israelites were banking on what the prophet Isaiah had said about the temple, claiming that it was beyond destruction and defilement (Isa 33:20). After all, the Jerusalem temple had withstood one potential invader after another and had stood even when the Assyrian army bore down on Jerusalem from the north. But now that Jerusalem was at the mercy of the Babylonians, its temple was in immanent danger of destruction. Some say Jesus had Jeremiah's sermon in mind when he saw people desecrating the Jerusalem temple years later and remarked, "You have made it a den of thieves." No wonder the prophet said that sort of temple worship should be abolished.

Further, Jeremiah called for an end to the practice of sacrifices, joining with contemporary prophets then for a virtual chorus against the rituals of burnt offerings. His reasoning was that animal sacrifice was not an original part of the Mosaic faith at all but a pagan rite adopted from other religions. Like the prophet Micah, he called for sacrifice to be replaced with obedience. His own words express it so much so more eloquently: "Thus says the Lord of hosts, the God of Israel—The day that I brought your ancestors out of the land of Egypt, I did not speak to them or command them concerning burnt offerings and sacrifices. But this command I gave to them, 'obey my voice and I will be your God and you shall be my people'" (7:21-23; 30-31).

Finally, Jeremiah did something absolutely unthinkable for a Jew; he struck out against Israel's status as a chosen nation. Wasn't that treason? Yet it was something that had to be said. The Israelites considered themselves invincible because of their covenant relationship with God. But they had forgotten something terribly important. Their covenant was both reciprocal and conditional; that is, it said that God's blessings were dependent on their faithfulness. That's when the prophet zeroed in on Israel's broken covenant relationship with God as the reason for that nation's loss of any special status before the Lord: "This is the nation that did not obey the voice of the Lord their God, and did not accept discipline; truth has perished," he said. Jeremiah then concluded: "The Lord has rejected and forsaken the generation that provoked his wrath" (7:28-29).

Reaction to the prophet's earthshaking temple sermon was both swift and predictable: "When Jeremiah had finished speaking all that the Lord had commanded him to speak to all the people, then the priests and the prophets and all the people laid hold on him saying, 'You shall die.'" Had the prophet gone too far with his criticism of the temple and its meaningless religious practices?

A lynching style mob awaited the prophet at the temple gate and a trial took place right then and there, with priests and prophets serving as prosecutors and city officials acting as the jury (26:17-23). But despite the charges leveled against him, Jeremiah refused to back down. He simply reaffirmed that he'd acted as God's spokesperson and repeated his call to repent (26:12-13).

Then something marvelous happened as the defense cited other prophets besides Jeremiah who also had called for the destruction of Jerusalem. Among them was the respected prophet Micah. When people heard such a defense they released Jeremiah and let him go free (26:24). But just to show how close he came to dying that day, the same mob had just killed another prophet named Uriah for saying virtually the same thing that Jeremiah had said about the Jerusalem temple. Unfortunately Uriah became so frightened that he ran away to Egypt and had to be brought back to Jerusalem in humiliation. In contrast to him, the way Jeremiah stood his ground was striking.

My prayer is that God shall grant Christians today the same kind of courage to speak out against those things that stand in the way of true worship. Recently I had an experience that reminded me of the dangers people face as they proclaim the truth of God's word. The International Mission Board asked me to translate Japanese correspondence between a missionary in Karbarask Russia and a friend in Tokyo Japan. It turned out to be nothing more than several innocent letters between two friends. But when I asked a fellow missionary why the mission board wanted to know what was in those letters, I learned that the missionary in Russia who wrote them had been murdered. What a shocker that was! Never before had I been so close to one who was killed for giving a gospel witness. It made me realize that even in the twenty-first-century believers must have the courage to call for a return to the true spiritual content of their faith regardless of the cost.

Jeremiah was willing to risk all to do just that. Are we?

Chapter 16

The Pain of God

A famous Japanese theologian named Kanamori captured Jeremiah's God in a book called *Theology of the Pain of God* (Wipf & Stock Publishers, June 2005). It's a form of doloroso theology that permeates Japanese Christianity and reflects the pain of living as a Christian in a non-Christian land. People there understand Jeremiah's God because they understand his pain. The author's thesis is that it is only through one's own pain that a believer comes to know the true meaning of the cross.

"My joy is gone, grief is upon me, my heart is sick," God says to Jeremiah in 8:18. Here, the prophet depicts God's pain with rare poetic sensitivity as he relates how deeply saddened the Lord is at the moral and spiritual plight of his people. The sight of the Holy City in ruins had brought the Lord God to tears.

Is it possible for God to feel such pain? Clearly, the writers of Scripture thought so. Remember Matthew's picture of Jesus weeping over the Holy City, "Jerusalem, Jerusalem, the city that kills the prophets and stones those who are sent to it! How often have I desired to gather your children together as a hen gathers her brood under her wings!" (23:37). Luke records it similarly, "As he came near and saw the city he wept over it saying, 'if you, even you, had only recognized on this day the things that make for peace!" (19:42).

The reason for God's pain was that he identified with the suffering of his people. Jeremiah makes that clear in chapter 8 with the following words, "For the hurt of my poor people I am hurt; I mourn and despair has taken hold of me"(8:21). Jeremiah's God wasn't some distant and unapproachable entity judging the world in detachment. He was intricately involved in human history and shared the joys and sorrows of his people. The Lord was saddened over the casualties of war and distressed that the Israelites defeat had brought an intrusion of enemy forces. More importantly, he grieved over their depraved moral and spiritual condition and deplored their broken relationship with the divine. Normally people think of God in terms of goodness, justice, wisdom and unity. But as the respected Old Testament scholar Abraham Heschel says, "God does not reveal himself in abstract absolutes but rather in a personal and intimate relation to the world."

I'm reminded of an evangelistic meeting I once conducted for a small Baptist congregation at the base of Mt. Fuji. It was a place of incredible beauty where one could stand at any point in the city and look up at the snow line of that famous mountain. We had an exceptionally good meeting that week and when services ended, the pastor took a group of us to a parishioner's house for prayer and thanksgiving. After a delicious meal, he motioned for a chorus to come out from behind a curtain and sing. They sang the familiar Japanese hymn *I Have No Hope But Jesus* so beautifully it brought tears to my eyes. But the words of that hymn became even more meaningful when the pastor explained that everyone in the chorus was blind. For who better than they, could understand that God shares our pain and offers hope for tomorrow.

Jeremiah's Pain

Jeremiah gives an unforgettable description of his own pain in the seven passages that we call his confessions or lamentations: Actually I prefer the word confessions because confessing is something I do daily. However, these Scriptures have the three characteristics of a traditional Old Testament lament. First, they begin with a definition of the crisis, second, they register the believer's complaint and third, they end with an expression of confidence that God's help is on the way. In one sense that's a description of the entire book of Jeremiah but for this study we shall concentrate on the following passages that scholars have identified as Jeremiah's laments.

The first lament is a cry of pain at the news of a plot against the prophet's life. Jeremiah was warned that his life would be in danger unless he quit prophesying (11:18-23). Imagine that! Under no circumstances would the prophet permit such a threat to silence his message. That was completely out of the question! Can you picture a preacher not preaching, or a prophet not prophesying because his life has been threatened? Remember what Jesus said when the Pharisees demanded that he order his disciples to stop preaching, "I tell you, if these (disciples) were silent, the stones would cry out" (Luke 19:40).

The problem was that these threats were not just some idle words of a few disgruntles. They came from the people that Jeremiah loved and trusted: friends and relatives in his hometown of Anathoth. But isn't it usually true that the people we know and love the most are the very ones most likely to betray us? Remember David's hurt when he was betrayed by his closest friend, or Jesus' anguish upon learning that one of his own disciples turned him over to the authorities? Again, who could forget Caesar's cry of distress that echoed through history when he looked at his companion in disbelief and cried out, "You too, Brutus?" We've all had similar experiences and can identify with Jeremiah as he poured out his heart to God in that moment of hurt and pain.

The second lament poses a question that pervades the Old Testament from the book of Job to the book of Psalms: "Why do the wicked prosper?" (12:1-6). It is an issue so important that the very first Psalm dealt with it head on.

I shall never forget an international phone call from Lois's family that came late one night in Tokyo, reporting her father's death. Her father was a towering German Jew from the old country who used to gather his children around him at night and read God's word in his native tongue. He had a booming voice that echoed throughout their small town when he talked on the telephone. And when he was well into his nineties the family missed him one day and after searching for hours finally found him up a pecan tree at the corner of the porch. He'd climbed there to meditate, he said. When the phone call came that night in Tokyo, Lois asked her sister if her father had said anything before he died. "Nothing important," she replied. "He just said the words 'Psalm 73,' that's all." Nothing important? Why it's one of the most important passages in God's word! Psalm 73 is the psalm that deals directly with the question of unjust prosperity and in vv. 16 and 17 concludes, "When I thought how to understand this, it became a wearisome task, until I went into the sanctuary of God, then I perceived their end" (73:16-17).

Jeremiah's third lament questions the reason for his birth (15:10-12). People do that sometime, you know. They become so despondent over life's problems that they shout out the wish they'd never been born. Jeremiah was like that, so wrapped up in his own problems that he used the personal pronoun in this lament a total of sixteen times in fewer than four verses. Had he forgotten that God's prophets were to lose self in the ministry of his word?

In the next lament Jeremiah sobs: "I sat alone." In other words he said, "I'm lonely!" (15:15-21). Who isn't? We all know what it means to be lonely. People often experience loneliness even in today's shopping malls with crowds milling about. Obviously that says the problem isn't external but internal. Jeremiah's condition was even worse. It was a loneliness that came from being cut off from the Lord of Life. Notice God's remedy: "If you turn back—I will make you to this people a fortified wall of bronze; they will fight against you, but they shall not prevail over you, for I am with you." It's the same promise that God gives to all who in their loneliness turn to him in faith.

Jeremiah's painful struggle with spiritual dryness is the next lament (17:14-18). What pastor has not wrestled with that problem? Listen to the prophet's cry of anguish, "See how they say to me, 'Where is the word of the Lord?'" In other words, people were saying that his prophecy was flat and were complaining that he was not communicating to them God's word. It's what writers call a writers block. All ministers, prophets and believers struggle with it as they experience dry periods during their ministry. I know about it first hand; sometimes I can sit down at the computer and the words fly so fast I cannot write down everything. On other occasions I can sit there for hours, even days, with no inspiration at all. But notice how Jeremiah's lament says that he began to heal when God gave him something to do: "Thus said the Lord to me; Go stand in the People's Gate, by which the kings of Judah enter and by which they go out, and in all the gates of Jerusalem, and say to them, Hear the word of the Lord" (17:19-20).

Martin Luther expressed the same sentiment when he said he went visiting when he didn't know what to preach about.

In yet another lament Jeremiah struggled with the problem of ridicule: "I have become a laughingstock all day long; everyone mocks me." Is there anything worse than becoming the laughingstock of the very people whose confidence one seeks? (20:7-13). It's said that once when Abraham Lincoln was accused of being two-faced he replied: "If I were two-faced, why do you think I'd choose to show you the face you see now?"

Now, for the final lament! If you expected that to be one of victory, you were mistaken. If anything, it is the worst of all because it leaves the prophet in a state of deep depression (20:14-16). Some scholars say Jeremiah was depressed because he'd expected the Lord to destroy his enemies. What a pitiful thought!

Frankly, reading such intimate confessions of the respected prophet makes one feel guilty, almost like an intruder. These are Jeremiah's innermost confessions of loneliness, pain and hurt. It's as though we, as readers, are trespassing his private space and treading where we don't belong. This isn't the side of spiritual leaders that we often see and certainly not something we freely reveal about ourselves. But aren't Jeremiah's struggles the same ones we all experience at times: loneliness, rejection, ridicule, dryness, inadequacy and yes, depression? A part of the prophet's greatness is that he recognized such problems in his own life and dealt with them.

Balm of Gilead

But let's not leave the prophet's pain here. I purposely chose to deal with Jeremiah's suffering in the context of God's own pain and his promise of healing.

The immortal words of chapter 8 say it best, "Is there no balm in Gilead? Is there no physician there?"(8:22). Gilead was a place east of the Jordan where people went for their medicines. Herbs found there were famous throughout the Middle East for their healing powers. Resin from the balsam tree was used to apply to open wounds, and numerous other medicines from across the Jordan are mentioned throughout the Scriptures. But Jeremiah knew that the wounds of the soul were different. He cried out to the only one who could cure those when he said, "Heal me O Lord and I shall be healed; save me and I shall be saved" (17:14). Here the prophet proclaims the *Lord's presence* as the balm in Gilead that heals the sin-sick soul.

As chancellor at Seinan University in Fukuoka, Japan it was my responsibility to speak to thousands at the school's graduations in March each year. Normally that meant addressing over three thousand at the university and additional hundreds who came for the high school and middle school graduations. There were festivities on each of the school's five campuses at graduation time and as chancellor I had to speak at all of them.

But the graduation for which I spent the most time preparing was neither the one at the university nor those at the middle and high schools. My greatest challenge was the kindergarten. (The university maintained a kindergarten for the college students to do their practice teaching.) Children there were leaving kindergarten friends and teachers as they graduated kindergarten and prepared to enter first grade. I could see that they were terribly apprehensive about the changes ahead and desperately wanted to say something to help make their transition easier. The problem was that I'd known exactly what to say to university and high school graduates—that was easy—but those kindergarten children were my Waterloo. I just didn't know what to say to them. Finally, after numerous miserable failures, God showed me that all I needed to say to those precious little children was just to tell them that as they left one school for another, they would not be alone. It was a Christian kindergarten and I simply reminded the children what Jesus said when he left his disciples: "I am with you always." And would you believe it? When I said that, it was uncanny the way you could see tension lift from their faces. All they needed to know was that God would be with them, not only as they changed schools, but always.

Chapter 17

A Letter From Home

Can you imagine what it's like for expatriates facing a difficult crisis abroad to receive a letter from home? That's what happens to missionaries all the time! My wife and I arrived in Japan before the days of e-mail when foreigners had to go all the way to the central post office in downtown Tokyo to receive mail from home. In those days it took seven days for letters from the U.S. to reach Japan. But it was so exciting to have any mail from America that people would stand in front of their post office boxes, rip open their letters and read them right there, oblivious of the fact they were blocking others from getting their mail. It was just uncanny how those letters from family and church always seemed to come right at the time of some great need.

Jeremiah's amazing letter to the Babylonian exiles was like that. The first wave of captives must have been the most depressed body of people on earth as they were snatched from their homeland and taken to Babylon when Jehoikim's rebellion against Nebuchadnezzar failed around 597 BCE. They were lonely and frustrated, surrounded by a people, a religion and a culture that they did not understand.

The prophet's wonderful letter from home arrived just at that moment of crisis. Jeremiah was writing from Jerusalem, where he had avoided being taken into captivity. Judah's new king Zedekiah had even sent two envoys to Babylon with the letter to make sure it was delivered to the Jewish exiles.

If you thought epistles were limited to the New Testament you were mistaken. Not only was Jeremiah's letter to the captives one of the first epistles ever, it's what a major Old Testament scholar calls, "one of the most significant documents of the Old Testament."

Jeremiah's letter was addressed to the entire community of exiles in Babylon: the elders, the priests, the prophets and "all the people." Evidently the captives were permitted to move about freely because they had already organized themselves into a community similar to the one they left in Jerusalem. The prophet's letter was an official document addressed to everyone in that body of displaced people.

The Jewish exiles were facing a complex dilemma of whether to revolt against their captors or to put down roots and make Babylon their new home. A prophet among them, named Shemiah, was urging the former course of action: rebellion against the Babylonians. But Jeremiah called him a false prophet.

Jeremiah told the Babylonian captives to do exactly the opposite of what Shemiah had proposed. He advised them to put down roots and make Babylon their new home. He said they would be there a long time and urged them to do three things: first, he encouraged them to adapt to the new situation. "Build houses and live in them," he said, "Plant gardens and eat what they produce, take wives and have sons and daughters—multiply there and do not decrease" (29:5). Jeremiah said the exiles should make Babylon their new home.

Second, the prophet did something truly amazing. He advised the exiles to pray for their captors "Seek the welfare of the city where I have sent you into exile and pray to the Lord on its behalf, "he said. Isn't that just about the closest thing in the Old Testament to what Jesus said about loving one's enemies?

Lastly, Jeremiah challenged the exiles to improvise. That is, he told them to create new forms of worship that fit their new situation. In one of the most beautiful passages in all Scripture, the prophet said, "When you search for me you will find me; if you seek me with all your heart." In other words, he assured them they could find God even in enemy territory (29:13). The Babylonian captives did just that! Hungry for a place to pray and frustrated at the lack of any Jewish temples of worship in Babylon, the exiles followed Jeremiah's advice and developed a completely new form of worship, one that eventually changed Judaism and Christianity forever.

That new worship structure was called a synagogue, literally a fellowship of believers, that not only became the key to Judaism's survival during the Babylonian captivity but even remains central to Jewish life and worship in the twenty-first century. The synagogue also became the pattern for the early Christian fellowship known as the *ecclesia*. Jewish and Christian forms of worship today are outgrowths of what the Israelites improvised while they were captives in Babylon.

Improvising is what missionaries and national Christians do all the time! In missions terminology it's called indigenization, a word that means to create new forms of witness that fit the land. Most American church members would not recognize the unique architecture of churches that their fellow believers build abroad or the different forms of worship they follow. But if anything, God's presence is often more deeply felt there than it is in the so-called orthodox Christian West.

Finally, Jeremiah's wonderful letter to the exiles promised hope for the future, "For surely I know the plans I have for you, says the Lord, plans for your welfare and not for harm, to give you a future with hope" (29:11). It reminds one me of Paul's letter to the Ephesians. Remember what that great apostle wrote to his favorite congregation at Ephesus: "This grace was given to me to bring to the Gentiles the news of the boundless riches of Christ, and to make everyone see what is the plan of the mystery hidden for ages in God who created all things" (3:8-9).

A favorite theologian of mine, named Moltmann, tells of a life-changing encounter that precipitated his fresh new approach to the Christian faith. He was a nonbeliever when he was drafted into the German army at an early age and was devastated at having to surrender to the British the next year. He said his time as a prisoner of war during the three years that followed was one of deep depression. But he told how a military chaplain had given him a Bible one day that turned his life around. Eventually it caused him to become one of the worlds leading theologians. Today Moltmann's book that reflects the dynamic of his thought is one of the most profound books on theology ever penned. He called it *The Theology of Hope* (Harper & Row, 1967).

Unfortunately, at first not all of the exiles agreed with Jeremiah's advice to put down roots in Babylon and the group that was plotting a rebellion against their captors sent a scathing letter to the high priest in Jerusalem calling Jeremiah a madman. But as everyone knows, any new proposal is always a calculated risk for leaders worth their salt. When I accepted the position of chancellor at Seinan University, I was told to expect dissent but not to worry about it because the lack of disagreement was an even greater problem, often signifying one's ineffectiveness.

Jeremiah's advice soon won out among the exiles. When they found his recommendation to put down roots to be sound and followed what he said, they emerged from captivity stronger than ever.

Inevitably, it seems that people of faith always seem to emerge from adversity stronger! Suffering has a way of shaking up one's shallow way of taking God for granted. It forces believers to reexamine the content of their belief, to explore the mysteries of their faith and to contemplate the meaning of eternity. When they do that, God blesses and strengthens them just as he did the captives in Babylon so long ago.

Have you heard the story of how Robert Schumann's wife became a famous concert pianist after his death? She played his music so beautifully that people flocked to her performances and she became famous across the continent. But one night as she stood offstage waiting for her cue to perform, a stagehand whispered, "Mrs. Schumann, it is always so different when you play Schumann's compositions. How can you play his music so masterfully?" She reached into her handbag and held up a hand-full of letters that her husband had written to her while he was still alive. She told the young man that before each concert she would take out those letters and reread every word in order to feel his presence again. Then she said she could play his music just as he would have played it himself. "That's my secret," she said.

Jeremiah's letter of encouragement to the Babylonian exiles is like that. It's a reminder that people of faith always come out of adversity stronger when they read God's word and experience his power and presence in their lives.

Chapter 18

A New Covenant

A major highlight of my missionary career was when members of the Japan Baptist Convention announced that they'd reached maturity and adopted a new covenant of faith. Previously they had used a translation of the Hawaiian Baptist Convention's English language faith statement, but they desperately wanted something in Japanese that expressed their own unique understanding of the gospel. They had struggled for over ten years to come up with something acceptable to their member churches. It was such a thrilling experience to be present at the annual convention in 1977 when over four hundred delegates met at Amagi Sanso, the Baptist retreat center in the mountains south of Tokyo, and voted to adopt a confession of faith that bound believers and churches together in a new covenant bond with one another, and with their Lord.

The book of Jeremiah reaches a crescendo that echoes throughout Scripture with the promise of a new covenant of the heart (ch. 31). Here the prophet does a dramatic about face, turning from despair to hope with the passage that says, "The days are surely coming, says the Lord, when I will make a new covenant with the house of Israel and with the house of Judah" (31:31). In so doing, Jeremiah joined a host of other prophets heralding a new direction in the spiritual life of God's people.

Some say Jesus had Jeremiah's new covenant in mind at the Last Supper when he held up the cup and said, "This is the new covenant in my blood" (1 Cor 11:25; Luke 22:20). Again, the book of Hebrews quotes Jeremiah's covenant passage verbatim in its most crucial chapter 8. Other New Testament writers refer to the new covenant repeatedly with such passages as the one in 2 Corinthians 3:5-14.

Also, Bible scholars claim that Jeremiah's new covenant is directly responsible for the two major divisions of the Old and New Testaments, the old covenant and the new covenant.

Generally people have to reach rock bottom before they begin to heal; and that is precisely what happened to the Israelites when Jerusalem's fall to the enemy cast a dark shadow over that once proud nation. Large numbers of its citizens were taken into captivity and endured innumerable difficulties as they were surrounded by a culture and a religion that they did not understand. Not only were they despondent and pessimistic; there was good reason for their despondency and their pessimism.

Chapter 30 makes a dramatic turn with God's promise to restore the fortunes of his people: "I will restore the fortunes of my people, Israel and Judah, says the Lord, and I will bring them back to the land that I gave their ancestors" (30:3). The poems that follow move from desperation to hope as he continues, "I will restore health to you and your wounds I will heal" (30:17). Still another Scripture depicts the Israelites' journey back to God with one of the most beautiful passages in God's word, "I have loved you with an everlasting love; therefore I have continued my faithfulness to you. Again I will build you and you shall be built O virgin Israel" (31:1-14). Finally, the great Old Testament prophet anticipates John's New Testament description of a new Jerusalem that would be built, not on the ruins of the old, but a wonderful new city which God would create especially for his people.

Next, the prophet introduces the nature of the new covenant, promising that it would differ drastically from the old one made at Sinai (31:27-34). Instead of the negative legalism of the old covenant, Jeremiah said the new covenant would abound in love and mercy. He then listed its five characteristics:

Grace: First, he said the new covenant would center in grace rather than in law. "It will not be like the covenant that I made with their ancestors when I took them by the hand to bring them out of the land of Egypt" (31:31). He even promised that the new covenant would pardon those who broke the old one.

Internal: Secondly, the new one would be an internal covenant, written on the heart, or, as Scripture puts it, "I will put my law within them, and I will write it on their hearts" (31:33). Paul describes it in 2 Corinthians as a relationship with God: "written not with ink but with the spirit of the living God, not on tablets of stone but on tablets of human hearts" (2 Cor 3:3). Henceforth God's people would not serve him out of fear but from a burning desire that sprang from within.

Individual: Again, the new covenant would be personal rather than corporate. (31:34). That means Jeremiah foresaw a covenant no longer exclusively for the Jews nor for any one race or nationality. Some say he envisioned a mission to the Gentiles. I'm convinced that Jeremiah would not be at all surprised by today's world missions ministry. Can't you just picture the prophet working side by side with missionaries and nationals in a global ministry to Japan and the world! Whether intentional or unintentional, the prophet's personal and individual covenant envisioned a future world mission that reached beyond any one nation, race or social class (Eph 2:11-22).

Infused: Further, the new covenant would be one divinely infused. That is, the negative "You shall not" passages in Exodus would be replaced with positive ones that stated, "I will put forth; I will forgive." Note the unmistakable change in emphasis from the believer to YHWH.

The description of an infused new covenant reminds me of numerous blood transfusions that I witnessed and participated in over the years. In the early years of my ministry the donor and the patient were placed side by side on two hospital gurneys and connected by a small plastic tube. As one watched the blood flow between the two, the patient's countenance would change visibly as new blood replaced the old. First, the fingers and toes would turn a healthy pink. Then the arms and legs would take on new life. Finally the cheeks would glow from the healthy new blood that flowed throughout the patient's body. The change was nothing short of miraculous. I miss seeing that transformation today as patients are hooked up to plasma contraptions right from the moment they enter the hospital. But one can never forget the physical change those former transfusions wrought.

To me they depicted the spiritual change that people experience when they enter into a new covenant relationship with their Lord.

Permanent: Finally the new covenant would be a permanent one. Or, as Jeremiah put it, "I will make an everlasting covenant with them, never to draw back from doing good to them" (32:40).

Jeremiah then did something remarkable! He was so confidant Israel would be restored that he bought a piece of property in the enemy occupied city of Anathoth, just north of Jerusalem. And how scholars love the account of that transaction, recorded in great detail in chapter 32! It provides valuable insight into the nature of business negotiations in ancient Palestine, even providing a record of the property price, a description of the deed signing, a statement of the number of witnesses required to make it legal and disclosure of the earthen jar that was used to store the documents. But most notably, the passage closes with those unforgettable words, "Fields shall be bought for money, and deeds shall be signed and sealed and witnessed—*for I will restore their fortunes*, says the Lord" (32:44).

The section ends with a wonderful passage hidden deep in the book of Jeremiah that anticipates the exiles' triumphant return from Babylon (ch. 50). "They shall ask the way to Zion, with faces turned toward it, and they shall come and join themselves to the Lord by an everlasting covenant that will never be forgotten." What a prophet! What a message!

Jeremiah's new covenant questions our own relationship to the Eternal. It asks if ours is a covenant of the heart, born of a dynamic personal experience of faith, instituted by God, founded in grace and destined to last forever? If it is, we can be sure God will bless us too, both individually and collectively, and grant a faith experience not unlike that which shook the ancient Israelites to the core, enabling them to emerge from adversity stronger than ever.

The word covenant is especially meaningful to Japanese Baptists because they trace their beginnings to a student covenant band that dates back to the 1870s. A professor named James had come from America to teach English at a boys' school in Kumamoto and was using the Bible as a text for his course. At one point his class of boys became so convicted by what they read that they professed their new faith and asked to be baptized. But James had to refuse, saying that he was only a layman and unqualified to perform the rite of baptism. Unable to find anyone who would agree to baptize them, the boys climbed a mountain behind the school after classes one day and when they reached the peak, they stopped and wrote out a covenant of faith. They slashed their wrists, and in lieu of baptism signed the covenant with their blood.

Once parents and school officials heard what happened, the students were severely reprimanded. They were disbanded, forbidden to continue their new faith, and sent to different schools across the nation. But guess what? Everywhere these dedicated young people went, they signed new faith covenants and began churches and Christian schools with such a forceful witness that the Christian faith spread rapidly across the nation. The place where it all began on the southern island of Kyushu is now the center for our Baptist work in Japan. The university where I taught has strong ties to the Kumamoto band and their covenant theology characterizes the school spirit there to this day.

Pray that our commitment to God today may be like Jeremiah's new covenant: signed with the blood of obedience and uniting believers to one another and to their Lord with a mutual faith for all eternity.

Appendix

A Unique Theological Heritage

"Tell It To The Church"

This study of Baptist theology is aimed at rediscovering the meaning and thrill of being both Christian and Baptist in the twenty-first century. Admittedly, this is an age when churches are dropping denominational labels for a new ecumenism and I need to assure you at the outset that I'm wholeheartedly in favor of the ecumenical movement and support participation in its ministry to the community and the world. But just as it's true that people do so much better relating to others when they're confident of their own identity, congregations that are sure of who they are and what they believe are better equipped to join others in a united ministry of fellowship and witness. That's what Japanese Baptists do beautifully. They belong to the interdenominational National Christian Counsel of Japan but continue to hold tenaciously to free church principles that distinguish them as Baptists. They never tire of hearing about the way Baptists led the struggle for religious liberty in the past and how they continue to stand for peace and freedom in the present.

Martin E. Marty, former editor of *Christianity Today*, once wrote a surprising article in that journal called "Baptistification Takes Over" (2 September 1983) that reported a new popularity of Baptist beliefs among Catholics, Methodists, Presbyterians and numerous other churches. Basically, it said to me that Baptists can be both proud of their unique theological heritage and at the same time participate in an ecumenical movement of worship and witness with other Christians.

What is so appealing about Baptist theology that makes it attractive, even to people of other denominations? This study proposes to examine the origin and nature of Baptist doctrines and to evaluate how conflicts over such beliefs continue to refine and redefine their faith today. This first section will trace the origins of Baptist Theology. The second one will take a fresh look at both the beliefs Baptists share with other Christians and those they hold separately. Then we'll close with a review of the controversies that continue to change Baptist doctrine and consider a prospectus for the future.

First, where did Baptist theology originate? The answer is that it came from a variety of sources. In addition to claiming the Bible as the primary source of their beliefs, Baptists gained important principles of faith from the mainline Protestant reformers: Luther, Calvin and Zwingli. They also adopted critical principles of faith from the Anabaptist radical reformers across Europe; and from English dissidents who carried the reformation to new levels in Great Britain. Furthermore, early Baptist pioneers in America gave the church a new vision of ministry and missions that has characterized it through the years. Baptists drew from each of these seventeenth and eighteenth century reform movements for a dynamic theology that centered in the importance of individual believers and the autonomous nature of the church.

Martin Luther laid the foundation for a believers' church with his two principles of *Sola Fide* and *Sola Scriptura*. *Sola Fide* affirmed that the sole condition for salvation was faith alone and *Sola Scriptura* declared that the Bible itself, not a religious institution, was the sole authority for the church. The thrilling story of how Luther took on the institutional church in the sixteenth century continues to inspire Christians even now. First, in the year 1517 he wrote out his opposition to the established church and nailed that document to the Castle Gate Church at Wittenberg. Four years later, when presented with a pile of his pamphlets scattered across a table at the Diet of Worms, he refused to recant what he had written. "Here I stand," he said, "I cannot do otherwise." Not only did he refuse once in German; he repeated what he'd said again in Latin. Luther then made Romans one seventeen come alive for Christians everywhere with his reformation cry of *justification by faith*. Although Baptists were not officially a part of the Protestant Reformation, the emphasis on the believer rather than on the institution gleaned from Luther and other reformers, has been at the heart of Baptist theology ever since.

Anabaptist radical reformers gave Baptists the principle of *believer's baptism.* The Greek prefix *ana* means "to repeat" and Anabaptists were called re-baptizers because they did baptize people twice. That is, they baptized those who had already been baptized as infants.

The problem with infant baptism was much more complex than a matter of biblical interpretation. The issue was political as well; governments in those days had made the baptism of infants a requirement for citizenship. Children were not automatically granted citizenship by virtue of where they were born; they had to have a document from the state church certifying that they were baptized as infants. That was true even of the Calvinistic government in Geneva, which severely punished Anabaptists for re-baptizing in that state.

Punishment for the crime of re-baptizing was death by drowning, a form of execution designed to fit the offence of baptizing by immersion. The Anabaptist leader Felix Manz was the first to die by drowning in Geneva. Given a chance to recant, Manz had refused, shouting, "*Nochfolge Christi,*" "I'll follow Christ." Other Anabaptist martyrs across the continent followed, numbering into the tens of thousands, all shouting the same words, *Nochfolge Christi,* as they died for their faith. These reformers gave Baptists something far more important than doctrine; they left an indelible testimony as to what following Christ really means.

However, despite the similarity between Baptists and Anabaptists, Baptist historians consistently denied any direct relationship with Anabaptists for fear of being identified with the Munster debacle that had left a black mark against religious reform across Europe. Nevertheless, the sound theology of such Anabaptist giants as Balthasar Hubmaier and Hans Denk more than compensated for the tragedy at Munster. These dedicated Anabaptist leaders would be a credit to any church; anytime, anywhere. Also, who can forget that English Separatists went to an Anabaptist haven in Amsterdam to begin the first Baptist church in history? One feels that history suggests a much stronger connection between these two groups than most Baptist scholars have been willing to admit.

The Baptist principle of *local church autonomy* was born when British Separatists, who were fed up with the lack of true religious reform in their country, left England and began a new church in Holland. Reformation in Great Britain was a different breed from that elsewhere in Europe. Religious reform there began when the British king broke with the church in Rome over the right to marry his lover, Anne Boleyn. He established the church of England which gave religious reform in that country a political color right from the beginning. Following that, Parliament passed the Supremacy Act in 1534 that made government intrusion into every aspect of church life so stifling that at one point pastors were told what topics to preach about for their Sunday sermons. As a result, ground swells of reform were everywhere, just beneath the surface, waiting for a chance to break out.

Something simply had to be done! Two groups of scholars, one at Oxford and one at Cambridge, could no longer remain silent and began an open struggle against the religious oppression in their country. One group, led by Cambridge University professor Thomas Cartwright, advocated radical changes within the church itself. He courageously attacked the government's right to appoint pastors and questioned the true nature of the church. He then led the call for a return to the apostolic pattern of congregational rule, citing the New Testament church as a true model for the church in any age.

The second group of believers that struggled against state church oppression were called Separatists. They were so named because they advocated a complete break with the Church of England. As early as 1528 Robert Brown wrote a pamphlet, titled *A treatise of reformation without tarrying for Anie*, in which he called for an immediate separation from the state church. He cited his favorite Scripture, Matthew 18:17 ("Tell it to the church"), as the source of authority for local congregations to make decisions concerning their own affairs. Consequently, that passage became a Baptist slogan, for many years to come.

Francis Johnson was charged with treason, by the state church of England, when he wrote a confession of faith that expressed the

Separatist Baptist principles. Subsequently, the persecution against Separatists that ensued caused some churches to leave England in search of religious freedom. The Gainsborough Church, headed by pastor John Smyth, was one entire congregation that boarded a ship and left for Holland in order to find a place where they could worship according to their own beliefs.

Once in Amsterdam, pastor John Smyth constituted the Gainsborough congregation into a Baptist church in the year 1609. Since there were no other Baptists nearby to assist in the church organization, pastor Smyth first baptized himself by pouring water over his own head. He then baptized other members of the congregation in like manner, creating the first Baptist church in history. Let's call it, Amsterdam First Baptist.

Two years later Thomas Helwys broke with John Smyth and returned to England in 1611. He began the first General Baptist Church just outside the wall of London and called it Spitalfield Baptist Church. Later a Southwark congregation became the first Particular Baptist church in England in the year 1616. It was named the Jacob-Lathrop-Jessie church after its first three pastors. Thereafter, Particular Baptists dominated the scene in early British Baptist history. The two strains of British Baptists, known as General and Particular, were so named because of their differing views on the atonement. General Baptists accepted the Armenian theology that taught Christ died to save all people and Particular Baptists were Calvinists who believed that Christ died for the elect only.

Now, fast-forward to America where Roger Williams gave Baptists the theological principle called *freedom of conscience.* Unable to adapt to the stifling theocracy in Massachusetts, Williams challenged its strict Puritan rule and as a result was banished from that territory in the year 1635. He proceeded to Rhode Island and there began the first Baptist church in America as "a shelter for people distressed in conscience." That church, named Providence Baptist was founded in the year 1638. And, wonder of wonders, even today U. S. school history texts credit Roger Williams and other early Baptists with giving this nation's early founding fathers democratic principles that profoundly influenced the Declaration of Independence and the U. S. Constitution.

Lastly, we turn to the origins of an *evangelistic outreach ministry* that influenced Baptists in America. No one captured that theology better than Georgia's own Daniel Marshal. By the year 1700 there were only fourteen Baptist churches in all of America, nine of them in the New England states. Yet, less than a century later they could be found all the way across the early U. S, from the New England States in the north to Virginia, North and South Carolina and Georgia in the south, as the Baptist witness exploded into one new area after another. Georgia is a good example of what happened. If you've never visited the site of the Kiokee Baptist church that Daniel Marshal began just eighteen miles from Augusta in 1772, you should. Originally it was a log cabin style building, filled with bullet holes, in the woods just outside of Appling Georgia. And, if you've never listened to the stories people in the area tell about how pastor Marshall rode horseback all the way from Augusta, and endured severe persecution to begin the first Baptist church in Georgia, you should. The story of his arrest on one occasion reads like something out of a popular novel. It tells how pastor Marshall was on his knees praying one day when he felt someone grip his shoulders and say, "You're my prisoner!" That day he was arrested for preaching the gospel and a friend, who accompanied him to his trial before the magistrate in Augusta, told how he was ordered never to preach again but replied to the judge, "Whether it be right to obey God rather than men, judge ye." Later, the very constable who arrested Marshall was so moved by what happened, he converted to the Baptist faith and was baptized at the Kiokee Church. Kiokee Church History records how he later volunteered for Christian service and was ordained to the ministry by pastor Marshall. Needless to say, Marshall's ministry and the Kiokee Church portray the kind of evangelistic zeal that has characterized the Baptist witness ever since.

What do these early beginnings have to do with Baptists today? This is an age of mega churches and of the theology of secularism when churches are struggling to blend in with society rather than stir up the waters. The Separatists' struggle to begin a church that was separate and different even to the point of entire congregations leaving their country in search of freedom seems utterly remote to the problems of the twenty-first century. But is it?

Once in Japan when I was working with a committee to draw up a handbook for our Baptist churches, we were shocked to discover that the word church society had been translated into Japanese as company. Just think of it—the Christian church as a company, a legal corporation formed to transact business like any secular organization. However acceptable the word company may be to describe business and academic organizations, it is completely inappropriate for a Christian church. What, then, is so unique about the church, we asked. We turned to the New Testament for three profound terms that describe the nature, mission and mystique of the church of God.

First, the word *ekklesia* (εκκλησια) that Jesus used for *church*, depicts a body of believers called apart from society the same way Jesus called his disciples to leave the world for a gospel ministry. The early churches were local congregations called out—the literal meaning of ekklesia—to preach, teach and baptize. Second, the word *covenant* (*diatheke;* διαθηκη) describes the church's relationship to God as a covenant like that which Israel had with the Lord in Old Testament times. That is, the relationship was reciprocal and conditioned, dependent on whether or not God's people remained faithful. The Old Testament scholar, Rawley explains that the theme of the Israelites' election for service was repeated throughout Scripture like the refrain of some great symphony. Finally, the New Testament term *body* (*soma;* σωμα) captures the church's role to become the person of Christ to the world. The word body signifies that the church, as the body of Christ, bears the pain of his suffering, shares the joy of his resurrection and proclaims his gospel of love and redemption. Furthermore, it depicts the church as a body of persons rather than a mere philosophical ideal.

It is hoped that this study of Baptist origins will remind believers who they are and challenge churches to reclaim their rich heritage of faith and mission for the twenty-first century.

Recently I read a book called *The God Factor* that reminded me how easy it is to forget who we are and why we're here. The author was reporting on a trip he made to Auschwitz in Poland where thousands of Jews perished during the war at that infamous death camp. He said that one day as he walked through the little town nearby, he met a group of men and asked if that was where they lived. The Catholic priest with them answered in the affirmative. He then asked if they were living there during the war. The priest pointed to a house across the street and said, "We lived just across from the camp, you could see it from our house" When they were asked to describe a typical day at the camp, the men told of constant, loud blaring music and sounds of marching all day long. Then, the author asked how they could sleep at night with all that going on. Guess what they replied? The priest said, "It was difficult at first, but then we got used to it."

How in the world does one get used to people dying by the thousands just a few feet away? Eventually, even the priest and the church failed to notice the pain and death anymore, because they'd gotten used to it. Incredible! But isn't the same thing happening again today as even the churches and the believers become so accustomed to the inhumanity, the immorality and the pain in our world, they fail to notice anymore?

One feels that what's needed today is a postmodern deconstruction and reconstruction twenty-first-century theology that replaces the current passive Christian church in America with a passionate body of believers called to be separate and different, to become true light and salt for an age threatened with meaninglessness.

"Tear Down Those Walls"

Christians have dealt with controversy from the very beginning and Baptists continue to struggle with divisive issues today in an attempt to refine and redefine who they are and what they believe. In his excellent book, *Not a Silent People* (Smyth & Helwys, 2000), Walter B. Shurden observes that, "The complexity and variety of Baptist thought is one reason, I suppose, why Baptist scholars have never written a book titled *Baptist Theology*." But I believe there is another, more disturbing, reason.

If you travel to Berlin, Germany, you will see a red line running through the heart of the city that marks the spot where the famous Berlin wall once stood. It's much like the yellow centerlines that mark the highways in America, except that it's red instead of yellow and it doesn't stay in the center. It zigzags back and forth, snaking along the streets and sidewalks well into the suburbs, apparently leading nowhere at all. But people who live there know what it stands for: a wall that once divided the people of that great metropolis right down the middle.

Can't you hear the Lord saying to Baptists today, "Tear down those walls"? It's time to tear down the walls of theology that continue to divide Baptists in much the same way that political ideologies once split the nation of Germany. It behooves believers everywhere to build on the lessons from past controversies; to put aside differences in their nuances of faith, and join together in the kingdom work, which our Lord has given to his people for this crucial time in history.

Early Skirmishes

Early on, British Baptists built walls of theology that divided them as they disagreed over matters of the atonement, Sabbath observance, eschatology, and the six principles of faith mentioned in Hebrews 6.

Atonement: General and Particular Baptists collided over the meaning of the atonement. The former, General Baptists, took the Armenian position that Christ died to save all people and the latter, Particular Baptists, held to the Calvinistic belief that he died to save only the elect.

Ordination: British churches that accepted the six principles found in Hebrews 6 as their articles of faith were called Six Principle Baptists. But they disagreed over one of those principles that led to the practice of ordaining all who were baptized.

Sabbath Observance: Seventh Day Baptists were what the name says they were: believers who claimed that Scripture taught the proper day for worship was Saturday instead of Sunday. However the seventh day movement wasn't confined to Baptists. It was so widespread that most denominations had members from both sides of the issue in their congregations.

Fifth Monarchy: Finally, disagreement over Daniel's apocalyptic teaching concerning God's universal rule, led to the establishment of a separate group called Fifth Monarchy Baptists. This group maintained that Christ would establish a fifth monarchy to succeed ancient monarchies of the Assyrians, Persians, Greeks and Romans. The problem was that they advocated using force to bring it to fruition. Sound familiar?

Perennial Debates

Next, Baptists in America built walls that divided them as they dealt with extreme positions on doctrines and the Christian life.

Landmarkism: The controversy over Landmark Theology has been around since 1854. That was the year James Pendleton used the word landmark to define the true marks of a Christian church, borrowing a term from Proverbs that says, "Do not remove the ancient landmark that your ancestors set up" (22:28). He identified seven landmarks that many Baptists still use for a rather *narrow view* of the Christian life. Baptists today are often surprised to learn that Landmarkism is responsible for the practice of closed communion and the opposition to alien immersion, both of which are still found in many churches.

Landmarkism also attempted to do for Baptists what apostolic succession had done for the Roman Catholic priesthood. That is, it sought to trace evidence for a Baptist exclusiveness all the way back to the New Testament. The problem wasn't just scriptural but had to do with the dubious heretical groups through which Landmark theologians searched for their ancestry in Christian history (Bogomills; Cathari, etc.).

One feels it's so much better to accept the fact that Baptists are a vital part of *mainstream Christian history.*

Fundamentalism: The fundamentalist controversy, that rocked Baptists early in the twentieth century, began as Frank Norris and others lashed out at biblical criticism and the kind of Darwinism popularized by the 1925 Scopes trial in Tennessee. Norris was a fiery pastor of the prestigious First Baptist Church in Fort Worth, Texas, who viciously attacked the liberal teachings of Baptist professors and Baptist institutions. However, extremists such as Frank Norris were not the only one who espoused fundamentalist ideas in those days. Many respected theologians also supported the fundamentalist movement, including Southern Baptist Seminary president E. Y. Mullins. Mullins authored the theology text I used as a student at Louisville seminary in the late forties. He also wrote for *The Fundamentals,* a fundamentalist publication that sold more than three million copies. According to theologian Walter Shurden, fundamentalism stressed the following five points: (1) divinely inspired and inerrant Scriptures, (2) deity of Christ and the virgin birth, (3) substitution atonement,

(4) Christ's bodily surrection, and (5) personal, premillennial, and imminent second coming.

The Baptist Faith and Message, approved in 1925, was originally a mild form of fundamentalism. However, it underwent numerous revisions in the sixties, eighties, and the year two thousand and became an increasingly conservative document, which excluded most moderate churches.

I'm convinced that Baptists could move beyond the fundamentalist controversy if they adopted a faith statement that allowed people to differ theologically. The more detailed a confession of faith becomes, the more people it *excludes*. A simple, *inclusive* statement of faith in the Lord and his salvation should be all that is needed to draw believers together and allow for the kind of theological diversity that's been a Baptist hallmark from the beginning.

Eschatology: The theology of last things has also been a point of contention among Christians and Baptists have come up with some real dillies on this issue. They revolve around the thousand-year period known as the millennium, mentioned in Revelation 20. Primarily, believers have disagreed over whether the *parousia*, or the second coming, would occur before or after the millennium. *Postmillennialists* believe Christ will return after the millennium that Christians have helped "bring in" through their ministry of evangelism. *Premillennialists* believe that Christ will return before the millennium, which they see as a time between Christ's second coming and the final judgment. *Amillennialists* understand the millennium symbolically, rather than as an actual period of history. My own take on all this is that the only thing we can be sure of about last things is that *nothing* is sure at all, except that Christ will come again and that the eternal hope found throughout God's word includes a future with the divine for all true believers.

Glossolalia: Holy Spirit movements have also divided Baptists over the years. This is not a new problem, of course, because Paul dealt with it in his first letter to the Corinthians: "In church I would rather speak five words with my mind, in order to instruct others, than ten thousand words in a tongue" (14:19). The words *charismatic* and *glossolalia* are from the Greek words *charis*, for gifts, and *glossais* for tongues. Paul used both words to describe gifts of the Holy Spirit in 1 Corinthians 12 and14.

The phenomenon of tongues speaking has been around forever. The philosopher Plato mentions *glossolalia* as part of the cultural expression in his day. But in the Christian church, the glossolalia or tongues speaking movement that broke out at Pentecost, had become such a problem by the time of Paul's letters that the apostle felt compelled to speak out against its abuse.

The problem with Pentecostal and the Charismatic movements is that not everyone experiences the Holy Spirit in the same way and to absolutize one type of experience above another is tantamount to limiting the Spirit of God. However, the phenomenal success of these movements worldwide should challenge all churches to make an encounter with the Holy Spirit a vital part of any worship experience. One recalls that no less a theologian than Schleiermacher emphasized the importance of feeling (Gefuhl) in religion. The ultimate test is whether such an experience manifests the fruits of the Spirit: love, joy, peace, temperance, compassion, good deeds, faithfulness, meekness and self-control (Gal 5:22-23).

Social gospel: The social gospel is another extreme movement that dates back to a giant among Baptist theologians, Walter Rauschenbusch. He taught that Christians should strive to make social and political changes believing God would bring them to pass, even though that might not occur during their lifetime. This is the movement that gave rise to the phrase, "Bringing in the kingdom," a slogan that was popular in Baptist churches during the last century. Problems with the social gospel arose, however, when an *overemphasis* on political action led to a neglect of the gospel's spiritual aspects.

Here again, the problem can be framed with just one word—abuse. Both social action and Holy Spirit movements are vital to the Christian faith but the abuse of either can destroy any true Christian fellowship. A balance between the two is essential for genuine Christian growth and a wholesome expression of one's faith.

Current Issues

Lastly, we turn to today's walls of discord that threaten to divide Baptists well into the future.

Inerrancy: First, Baptists are seriously divided over the literalist interpretation of Scripture that says every word in the Bible is true. It's called the *inerrancy debate.* Those who argue for the affirmative claim that all words and facts in the original Greek and Hebrew manuscripts are without error. However, questions that remain concerning the scientific and historical inaccuracies throughout Scripture are formidable. A more balanced approach to hermeneutics must look beyond mere words and facts to the spiritual truths that God's word conveys about God, salvation and life. This is called the dynamic theory of biblical interpretation.

The story is told of a Japanese samurai ruler in the sixteenth century who received a Bible from a missionary but was unable to read it because it was written in the Dutch language. The shogun was so anxious to know what the Bible said that he sent to Shanghai for an interpreter to come and read it to him in Japanese. Eventually one was found and brought to Japan. The shogun was elated and listened intently as the interpreter read the entire New Testament to him in Japanese. Then after remarking that Christianity was truly a great teaching, he turned to the people around him said, "I would like to see one of those."

Creationism: Baptists are also divided over whether to accept the Genesis account of creation or to go with Darwin's theory of evolution. But should this issue be that divisive, really? If one truly believes that the Lord of Scripture created all things, he or she should find no inconsistency accepting the scientific evidence that God created life to evolve, to grow and change, through the years. I like theologian Ted Peters's explanation in his book, *God, The World's Future* (Fortress Press, 2000): "Nothing was created all at once. Everything, including human beings, is on the way, so to speak. Furthermore, as earth's system continues to take in energy, we can expect still more relative activity in the future." "Creation is ongoing."

Gender: Another current debate is over the matter of gender. It is highlighted by two recent revisions to the *Baptist Faith and Message*. In 1998 article eighteen was revised to read, "A wife is to submit graciously to the servant leadership of her husband" and in the year 2000, article six was amended as follows, "While both men and women are gifted for service in the church, the office of pastor is limited to men as qualified by Scripture." However, the first amendment cites Ephesians 5 as a reference for male superiority in the home (5:22) but fails to mention the former verse, "Be subject to *one another* out of reverence to Christ" (5:21). The latter amendment on female church leadership cites 1 Timothy 2 in support of the opposition to women pastors (2:11-12) but completely overlooks the context of Paul's writing as a whole, especially the passage in Galatians that says, "There is no longer Jew or Greek, there is no longer slave or free, there is no longer male and female; for all of you are one in Christ Jesus" (3:28).

The same proof text method used to support the subjugation of women in the home and in the church could be, and was, used to support slavery in the past. In fact, that very proof text form of argument was used by southern slave owners to split northern and southern Baptists and form the Southern Baptist Convention in 1845.

Missions: Finally, the conflict over world missions that began with William Carey's appointment as a missionary to India, is still around today. Carey became the first Baptist missionary ever in January 1793, but not before enduring a nasty controversy over world missions. After his impassioned plea for the Nottingham Association in England to send missionaries to India, an elderly minister stood up and said, "Sit down, young man; if God wants to save the heathen he is God enough to do it without our help." But Carey responded with one of the greatest missionary sermons ever. He took his text from Isaiah: "Enlarge the site of your tent, and let the curtains of your habitations be stretched out; do not hold back; lengthen your cords and strengthen your stakes" (54:2). Carey concluded with those famous words that have inspired Baptists through the years, "Expect great things from God and attempt great things for God."

Today's thrilling new missions challenge is for former sending and receiving churches to join together as one in an unprecedented international movement of worship and witness. Baptists abroad have matured in every way—numerically, spiritually and theologically—and are developing exciting new forms of theology and ministry. I'm convinced that Baptists in America have much to learn from these new Christians abroad. Conversely, the young churches in former mission territories desperately need the support of a larger and more seasoned Baptist constituency in the West. I'm convinced that together these two could shake up our age with a spiritual awakening that surpasses the great Christian reform movements of the past.

Let's tear down the walls that divide Baptists and join together as one for the work of ministry and missions that God has given his people at this crucial time in history.

I like Calvin Miller's story about being distracted one Sunday by a little girl who was drawing something throughout his entire sermon. It seems that Miller always had a problem with children fidgeting while he spoke. But this little girl still held her picture when he greeted the family after church that day and curious to know what she had drawn, he asked if he could see it. The little girl proudly held up a picture that she had drawn of Miller in the pulpit preaching away, with a heavenly angel hovering just above his shoulder. Miller said that scene moved him to tears and caused him to see his ministry in an entirely new light.

My prayer is that this study may become a mirror that questions one's theological self-image and adds a new sense of objectivity and depth to his or her life and witness as a Christian.

"Saved by His Life"

The ambitious effort to draw together what Baptists believe reminds me of the final exam that I took for a theology course one furlough when I was doing research at Columbia Seminary in Decatur, Georgia. It was an excellent course and I had studied extra hard for that final test. But when the exam sheets were distributed and I saw that the entire test consisted of just one question, I almost fell over. What a question it was: "Write a statement of your own theology." It was at once the most disconcerting and the most remarkably helpful exam I've ever experienced because it forced me to take what the professor taught that year and use it to draw together my own theology in a way that I had never done before. That's what we're attempting to do with this study: confirm, verify and recommit to what we believe, both as Christians and as Baptists, in preparation for deeper and more effective lives of faith and service.

Thomas Aquinas and William of Ockham demonstrated two classic approaches to theology with deductive and inductive forms of reason that both supported the institutional church and called for its reform. These two methods of theology were called *via antiqua* and *via moderna*. Thomas Aquinas used the former, a deductive form of theology, to reason from the general to the particular in the effort to find a theology that would draw together reason and faith, philosophy and religion, and ultimately God and man. He even called his masterwork *Suma Theologia*, believing it to be the final word on theology for all time. But his theology ended up supporting the institutional church and its stranglehold on virtually every aspect of society in those days. That's because the church was where his theology began, with God's revelation to the institutional church.

However, William of Ockham at Oxford University used an inductive form of theology to do just the opposite. His method, called *via moderna*, was based on the philosophy of nominalism, and he reasoned from the particular to the general for a theology that ultimately brought about the Protestant Reformation. That's because his theology started with God's revelation to the individual, the believer, rather than the church. Baptist theology, needless to say, is in the tradition of the latter.

We begin with a survey of the beliefs that Baptists share with all Christians. They are principles sine qua non to the Christian faith that believers hold in every major denominational persuasion.

First, is the doctrine of scriptural authority. Not surprisingly all Christians begin their theology with the Bible as the source of God's revelation. It's Martin Luther's principle of *Sola Scriptura* or Scripture alone. New converts in Japan are always amazed to discover that the Old and New Testaments were written by multiple authors over thousands of years *yet contain the same gospel*. Paul reconfirms this truth with his passage in 2 Timothy: "All Scripture is inspired by God and is useful for teaching, for reproof, for correction, and for training in righteousness" (3:16).

I like the story of a new Japanese Christian who was so anxious to make Scripture the foundation for his life that he actually ate the Bible. Not all at once but gradually; he ate it one page at a time. That is, he would read one page and memorize it. Then, once he had made it his own he would tear that page out of the Bible and eat it. He continued doing this over a period of years until he'd consumed the entire Bible. While we're not required to actually eat the Bible like this man did, it's safe to say that theology begins and ends with the revelation that comes to God's people as they ponder the truths of his word.

Second, the doctrine of God is traditionally explained with monotheistic terms such as transcendent, sovereign, supreme and absolute. This is a reflection of the definitive statement issued by the Council of Nicaea in the year 325 CE, "We believe in *one God* the Father, *All-sovereign, maker of all things* visible and invisible." It's a concept of deity based on the Genesis account that God is creator and Lord, the source of life itself. Even the progressive philosopher-theologian Hegel defined God as *absolute*, an absolute spirit.

Unfortunately, such a monotheistic understanding of the divine is no longer a cut and dried given for the current day. This is a new age of pantheistic pluralism in which the understanding of God as absolute is under serious attack. Christians are once again called on to defend their faith in the one God of Scripture just as biblical writers had to do long ago. Pan means all and Pantheism says that God is the sum total of all that exists *but nothing more*. It rejects such words as absolute, transcendent and supreme to describe the divine.

However, I'm convinced that it would be a serious mistake to glibly abandon belief in the monotheistic creator Lord of Scripture. It is a teaching as unique and important to the current age as it was in the pluralistic age of Scripture. People are still moved by the teaching that not only is God creator, savior and Lord but that his continuing work of creation is the source of true salvation, life and happiness.

Orthodox Christianity also accepts the *Trinitarian* theology that describes God as three persons in one. Unfortunately, many forget that this doctrine is primarily about the unity of God rather than about the three different persons of Father, Son and Holy Spirit. It's an understatement to say that this is one of the hardest fought doctrines in Christian history, discussed at all seven church councils and finalized only after extended debate.

The *first person* of the trinity, God the Father, already described in connection with the doctrine of God, has to be seen as the ideal of a loving father. Otherwise the father image of God is easily misunderstood in an age of incompatible marriages and broken homes. Shusaku Endo, the famous Japanese Christian author, rejects the use of the word father for God because the father image in his country is that of an absentee, unloving, tyrant. Endo prefers to speak of the *Motherhood of God* instead. Next, the *second person* of the trinity, God incarnate in Jesus Christ, is another doctrine that dates back to the Council of Nicaea: "We believe—in one Lord Jesus Christ, the son of God, begotten of the Father, only-begotten, that is, of the substance (*homoousion*) of the father, *God of God, Light of Light, true God of true God, begotten not made, of one substance with the father.*" Significantly, the Greek word *homoousion* for same substance rather than *homolousion* for similar substance is used to make it clear that Jesus is of the same substance as God rather than one who is similar to or inferior to God. The two divine and human natures of Christ make him an expression of divinity with whom humans can identify. Again, the doctrine of the Holy Spirit, the *third person* of the trinity, was solidified by the Council of Chalcedon in the year 451 CE: "We believe—in the Holy Spirit, the Lord and the Life-giver, that proceeded from the Father, who with the Father and Son is worshiped together and glorified together, who spoke through the prophets." John's Gospel describes the Spirit as a *paraclete* (παρακλητος), literally one who adds a divine dimension to every aspect of one's life by walking beside the believer at all times.

A group of students at Seinan University in Japan set out one night to capture the Holy Spirit on film because they identified the third person in the trinity with the school spirit of their Christian University. They cut out a cross in the middle of a piece of cardboard and blew steam through the hole hoping it would form a white silhouette of the Holy Spirit, framing it against the darkness. They spent an entire night doing this and took over a thousand photographs but finally had to admit defeat. They concluded that it couldn't be done. But they came up with the next best thing the picture of a white steam cross hovering in the night darkness like a cloud of divine hope. They called it Seinan's school spirit and placed their picture of the Holy Spirit in that year's school album.

The theology of humankind is next. Christian theology has to have the highest view of human beings ever recorded because it captures the incredible sense of dignity and responsibility with which people are endowed from birth. It's a belief that centers in the *imago Dei*, the divine image, in the Genesis account that says, "God created humankind in his image, in the image of God he created them" (1:27). A prominent contemporary theologian named Moltmann, introduces yet another term to complement the word *imago Dei* that he calls *imago trinitatis*. It says that in addition to the way people are created to resemble God individually, they're also created to resemble him collectively. The author's own words describe it best, "Just as the three Persons of the Trinity are 'one' in a wholly, unique way, so, similarly, human beings are *imago trinitatis* in their personal fellowship with one another."

Another fundamental Christian doctrine is one that we have traditionally called sin. But here let's call it disobedience instead. As a new missionary to Japan, I was troubled to discover that the Japanese language has no words for either sin or guilt. There the word sin has to be translated with the legal term for crime, *tsumi*. This holds true even in Scripture. Of course, it means that sin is easily misunderstood in Japan to mean the transgression of a human rather than a divine law. That is true for the word guilt also; the same word, crime, has to be used for guilt as well. Therefore, the word sin is even more offensive in that language than it is in English, and frankly, during the forty-three years I was a missionary in Japan, I avoided using the word sin, or *tsumi*, altogether.

Augustine of Hippo's teaching that humankind has a propensity to sin comes close to a doctrine of original sin and John Calvin picked up on it for a strict deterministic view of predestination. *His Institutes* mince no words stating his position on the subject, "No one who wishes to be thought religious dares outright to deny predestination, by which God chooses some for the hope of life and condemns others to eternal death" (*Institutes* book III). However, Arminius, the Dutch reformer, countered saying, "Divine sovereignty is compatible with a real free-will in man."

But disobedience, rejection and rebellion are facts of life. Any responsible theology should affirm the importance of confessing one's disobedience to God and asking for forgiveness. One of the first sounds I remember hearing in Japan was that of a man running through our community at night beating two sticks together and yelling, "*Hi no Yojin!*" I knew it had to be something urgent, but I didn't understand what he was saying at first. Later, when I found out that he was warning people to "be careful for fires," I began to pay better attention to my lifestyle. It was a forceful reminder that theology would be equally irresponsible without a similar warning for people to be careful in their spiritual lives.

Logically, that which follows is the doctrine of salvation. Historically, there have been many views of the atonement as the means of salvation, including Anselm's satisfaction or ransom theory that alluded to the cross as payment for man's sin. Most present day theologians, however, hold that believers are reconciled by God's love rather than by some arbitrary legal transaction. No Scripture explains it better than the one in Romans 5 that says we're "saved by his life" (σωθησομεθα εν τη ζωη αυτου). That means we're not just saved by the cross but by the whole person of Christ: his birth, death and resurrection.

Of course, there's no denying that the cross is a universal symbol for salvation. Lois and I learned that in an unforgettable way when our son died in Japan of leukemia at age four and we purchased a tombstone for his grave. We were anxious to have something carved on that stone to reflect his simple faith and had chosen a lamb, thinking it would represent God's love for even the smallest child. But the Japanese stonecutter advised against it. He said the image of a lamb would likely be misunderstood in Japan because people there were not familiar with sheep and would consider them dirty animals. When we asked what he'd suggest, he replied, "I think you should use a cross because it's a universal symbol for the Christian faith." We agreed and are still convinced that the cross which marks our son's grave on the campus at Seinan Jo College in Kyushu is an adequate testimony to his childlike faith, both to Japan and to the world.

Lastly, we turn to the doctrine of eschatology. All Christians hold to some view of the eschaton, or last things, even though they may differ greatly concerning the specifics. Jesus' own eschatology centered in his teaching about the kingdom of God. However, as for the timing of its fulfillment, on occasion Jesus said no one knows when that will happen. "But about that day or hour no one knows, neither the angels in heaven, nor the Son, but only the Father" (Mark 13: 32ff). On other occasions he emphasized that the kingdom had come already in the hearts of those who believed. Thus, while believers live with an eschatological tension between the "not yet" and the "already" aspects of God's eternal kingdom, they have the wonderful promise of its ultimate fulfillment.

I'm reminded of the story about a missionary who was returning to the states on the same ship with a famous movie star who had been abroad for a brief tour of the Orient. When they reached San Francisco there were throngs of people waiting to greet the ocean liner.

The movie star, who was the first to debark, was carried away by the adoring crowd but by the time the missionary walked down the gangplank there was no one left to welcome him home. No one at all. As the missionary hailed a taxi and headed for his hotel downtown, he paused to thank God for a safe voyage. Then he asked the Lord why a movie star who'd been away only a few weeks received such a royal welcome yet there was no one to greet this missionary who'd spent a lifetime proclaiming the gospel abroad. The Lord replied ever so softly, "But my son, you're not *home* yet." There are many things confusing about the doctrine of last things but one thing is certain: Jesus clearly promised a place in God's eternal kingdom for all who believe.

Now we turn to those principles of faith, which are unique to the Baptist heritage. I like what Hershel Hobbs said about Baptists not having a second Bible that is different from the one other Christians use. Baptists believe in the same Bible and accept the same basic tenets of faith that all Christians affirm. However, in addition they hold to certain principles and practices concerning the Christian life that are unique to the Baptist tradition.

One principle of faith particularly dear to Baptists is the priesthood of the believer. Martin Luther used it in his *Address to the German Nobility* in connection with the first of three walls of institutionalism that he said the church needed to tear down. Historian Bill Leonard observes that, "Baptists place great emphasis on the Reformation doctrine of the priesthood of all believers, insisting that each individual may encounter God's grace directly, without clerical or ecclesiastical mediation." It's a doctrine that is sometimes misunderstood to mean every Christian is his own priest before God. But that's not the intent of the Scripture passage on which the doctrine is based in 1 Peter (1 Pet 2:9-10). The *plural* tense of the word priest in that passage says the believer's priestly role is a corporate one shared with other believers, a royal priesthood, "to proclaim the mighty acts of him who called you out of darkness into his marvelous light."

Next, Baptists hold that baptism is for believers only. That is, they believe baptism doesn't save a person but that it signifies one is saved already. In other words, baptism is neither a sacrament with the mystical power to save a person, nor a child's right of passage via infant baptism. Rather, it is a testimony to the believer's faith and to the Lord's saving presence in his or her life. It follows that if baptism is a sign rather than a means of salvation, there is no need for one to be rebaptized.

Baptists also specify that the correct method of baptism is by immersion, after the manner in which Jesus was baptized (Matt 3:13-17). The extent to which some Baptists go to carry out this teaching can be downright humorous at times. Most Japanese churches had no baptisteries when I first arrived on the mission field and I had to baptize people in everything imaginable. That included hastily made narrow steel tubs where the minister stood outside and had to get the candidate underwater the best way he could. Again I baptized in shallow creeks where the water was once only two feet deep and in the Japan Sea where waves were so fierce they once lifted the candidate and the minister high into the air but miraculously put us both down safely in an upright position. On one occasion I even baptized in a hot springs spa on Japan's northern island of Hokkaido in the dead of winter. But inevitably those were happy occasions for both the new believers and the churches. The sense of God's presence was always there.

At the pinnacle of Baptist theology is the doctrine of the church, defined as an *autonomous* body of baptized believers. Here, the word autonomous is critical because it reflects the way the New Testament Church, the *ekklesia*, administered its affairs. Ninety-three of the one hundred fifteen times this word for church is used in the New Testament it refers to a local congregation ("The church of God that is in Corinth," etc.). Separatists chose Jesus words, "Tell it to the church." as their slogan precisely because it referred to the principle of local church autonomy (Matt 18:17-21).

Separation of church and state was another hard fought doctrine that historically stood right next to the freedom of religion in importance for most Baptists. Unfortunately, many Christians have mistakenly interpreted the danger that this doctrine addresses as state control of the church when historically it has been just the opposite. The greater danger has always been *church control of the state.* A prime example of the latter is what happened in Christian history when the institutional church fought holy wars and used inhuman methods to punish dissenters in the name of God.

Baptists also hold that the Bible itself is the ultimate authority for our faith. They oppose the use of creeds as a set of doctrines to which believers must conform. That is, they insist on the right of every believer to interpret the Bible freely and independently. Many are surprised to learn that the *Apostles Creed*, often quoted in worship services, is neither of apostolic nor of especially ancient origin. The oldest confession of faith is believed to be the baptismal formula Christ used in the great commission (Matt 28:19). In his book *Our Baptist Tradition* (Smyth & Helwys, 2005), William Tuck relates an amusing incident about a seminary student who drew a cartoon of Jesus talking to Simon Peter at Caesarea. To Jesus' question, "Who do men say that the son of man is?" the cartoon has Peter replying, "Thou art the paradoxical Kerygma, the epistemological manifestation of the existential ground of ontological ultimacy." It points out the meaningless and vague nature of most creedal statements.

Finally, nothing has bound Baptists together more closely than the theology of world missions. They believe that God calls them to do something more than enjoy a comfortable life in the *Sanctorum Communio*. Baptists are convinced that Jesus' final commission in Matthew sends believers on a mission to proclaim the gospel to "*all nations*" (28:19), or as the gospel of Mark puts it, "to the *whole creation*" (16:15). The Japan Baptist Convention's mission statement captures the compelling nature of that mission as well as anything I know: "The church makes clear its *raison d'etre*, fulfills its true calling, becomes self-giving and reaps abundant blessings from God as it rises above self and launches out into the world. The Lord of the Universe desires that all men everywhere believe the gospel and receive eternal life. Therefore it is required that all who belong to Christ's body proclaim his gospel to the utmost parts of the earth."

In closing, one must never forget that theology, at best, is only a roadmap, or better still, a road. Granted, it points the way to a life of faith but ultimately it is the light of God's Spirit that enables one to see the road on a dark night.

I shall never forget what happened one dark night when I was out visiting for the church where I was pastor in Fredericksburg, Virginia. I had just started home on a lonely country road when suddenly everything turned black. The lights on my car had failed and I couldn't see a thing! I was unable even to pull over to the curb and had to stop there and then, right in the middle of the road. Since it was a seldom-traveled rural road, several hours elapsed before anyone came along to help. I finally got home in the wee hours of the next morning. But when people at church heard what happened they just laughed at me for not carrying an extra set of fuses for such an emergency. That's what we all do in this area, they said. And guess what! To this day I still carry an extra set of fuses taped beneath the dashboard on my car to use in an emergency.

That night in Fredericksburg I learned that not only do people need a road map to guide them to their destination, they need a light to see the road on a dark night. That's true of one's theology as well. Regardless of how logically correct and soundly orthodox one's doctrines may be, without the light of God's Spirit it's easy to lose one's way on those dark nights of the soul. My prayer is not just that your theology may be correct but that God's Spirit may always be present to show you the way home.